CANNONBALL MOMENTS

D0104581

CANNONBALL MOMENTS

Telling Your Story,
Deepening Your Faith

ERIC A. CLAYTON

LOYOLAPRESS.
A JESUIT MINISTRY
Chicago

LOYOLA PRESS.
A JESUIT MINISTRY
www.loyolapress.com

Copyright © 2022 Eric A. Clayton
All rights reserved.

Scripture texts in this work are taken from the *New American Bible with Revised New Testament and Revised Psalms* © 1991, 1986, 1970 Confraternity of Christian Doctrine, Washington, D.C. and are used by permission of the copyright owner. All Rights Reserved. No part of the *New American Bible* may be reproduced in any form without permission in writing from the copyright owner.

Cover art credit: natrot/iStock/Getty Images, Evgenii_Bobrov/iStock/Getty Images

ISBN: 978-0-8294-5436-9
Library of Congress Control Number: 2021947899

Printed in the United States of America.
23 24 25 26 27 28 29 30 31 Versa 10 9 8 7 6 5 4 3 2

For Ma, who read every word for as long as she could.

Contents

Introduction: A Spirituality of Storytelling

Kool-Aid is rarely considered a weapon.

But for me and my grandmother telling stories, many years ago, it was the only way to defeat the imaginary foul Conquerors, multicolored bird-like creatures that frequently terrorized my friends. Different-colored Kool-Aid would vanquish different-colored Conquerors, and so keeping a good selection of powdered packets on hand was a must for a five-year-old storyteller.

"Who's in our story today?" my grandmother would ask.

I would rattle off the names of my friends and some dangerous situation in which they might find themselves, and then my grandmother would begin. This small band of children was going on a hike one day when, out of nowhere, colorful clouds gathered and—Gasp!—Conquerors appeared from within, bent on wreaking havoc. Our heroes fought valiantly but never seemed to have quite the amount of Kool-Aid the moment required.

Not to worry. Eric (that's me) was never far away, Kool-Aid ready-to-hand to be sprayed on the unsuspecting Conquerors. Imagine a high-tech super soaker-type contraption.

And they all lived happily ever after.

I haven't seen a Conqueror or a Kool-Aid packet in a good many years, but I still revisit these conversations with my grandmother—Ma, as I called her—with some frequency. These stories hold a special place in my memory, in my formation. What began as silly childhood tales evolved into more serious stories: stories of proposals, weddings, and pregnancies; stories of sickness, sadness, and death; stories of travel, dreams, politics, and faith. These stories revealed to me what I found to be important, what mattered, and how I might respond. And they depended on a relationship with my grandmother that was woven together ever more tightly with more time and more stories. As I grew, I began to see myself in her stories, and as she aged, she was forced to live through mine.

Here the seeds of my spirituality of storytelling were planted.

Stories have the power to make us laugh, to console us, to expand our thinking and challenge our perspectives. Stories hold the power of truth, the power to sustain belief, and the power to topple structures of injustice.

Stories are powerful because they bring us together. They connect and heal us. They build bridges between adversaries, strengthen bonds among friends, and can even restore the broken pieces we collect of ourselves. They help us make sense of our own purpose and then give us the inspiration to seize it. This is the role stories have played throughout human history.

This is a book about storytelling. But it's also a book about spirituality. It's an attempt to marry the two ideas together. It's a spirituality of storytelling that uses the language and tools of Ignatian spirituality, a path that invites us to exercise our imaginations, to encounter that which is sacred in ourselves and in others through that very same power of imaginative storytelling. We might call it Ignatian storytelling. The legacy of a soldier-turned-saint, Ignatius of Loyola, and the spiritual tools presented in this book have been honed over the course of 500 years. Countless lives have been changed through their use.

No matter what name we use for God, no matter with which religious tradition—if any—we identify, no matter how we approach that which is sacred, we must pass through the gateway of storytelling. We absorb the stories of our time, culture, faith, and friends. And we reinterpret anew those stories for others. These stories are ultimately our attempt to make sense of our own lives and of the impact our lives have on others. Our efforts to wrestle with the biggest questions that life presents—questions of identity, meaning, justice, and love—are efforts to share stories with spiritual significance.

Storytelling is a process of self-discovery, self-acceptance, and personal and communal healing. Doing the hard work of realizing your story and how it relates to the stories of others is a journey of recognizing and claiming your unique potential. In committing to that work throughout this book, you will be challenged to strengthen how you relate to yourself, to others, to the world, and to God. This book is a retreat, an opportunity to set aside some sacred time and space for yourself to better understand the stories that make up your life, that are woven into the very fabric of who you are—and why they matter.

Learning to tell our stories is an exercise in deepening faith—faith in a God intimately at work in our lives and the lives of others. Faith in ourselves, too, that even in our darkest moments, we are enough; God has seen to that.

In uncovering these stories of self, you will undoubtedly uncover stories of others and your relationship to them. This is the great web of storytelling that makes up your life and connects you to other people, friend and stranger alike. To navigate this web, we will use three key questions—Who am I? Whose am I? Who am I called to be? These questions will organize this book's reflections.

Saint Ignatius of Loyola founded a religious order of Catholic priests and brothers, the Society of Jesus, more commonly referred to as the Jesuits. The stories of the Christian Scriptures inspired them in their work as educators, advocates, and missionaries—and continue to do so to this day. Saint Ignatius reminds us that, regardless of our spiritual tradition, we are inextricably bound to the stories that have preceded us. Our stories are written not in a vacuum but as a new chapter in an ongoing tale. We respond to what has gone before; we build on the foundation others have laid. To do so, we must nurture the humility to see our story as one of many, part of a larger narrative. Perhaps we call it God's story of creation.

Ignatius's own cannonball moment was violent and traumatic and a seemingly meaningless event. It wasn't until the injured soldier brought his story into dialogue with the stories of saints and sinners of the past that he began to make sense of his wound—and the new life he was being called to. It took courage, discernment, and trust.

As we proceed in this book, I will share my own stories with you, what I have learned and grappled with through the application of the storytelling tools given to us through Ignatian spirituality, and how I have discovered my own purpose through the stories that make up my life. I hope that, though unique to me, my stories will accompany you in a deepening understanding of self. Perhaps most significantly, I hope my storytelling serves as an ongoing exercise in a spirituality of storytelling that connects me to you, us to the world, the world to God. Through that connection, we more clearly see our unique value woven into the universe.

The spiritual principles we will explore in the chapters that follow point to a foundational claim of Ignatian spirituality: God is in all things. Every person, every plant, every moment, every idea—God is there. Everything, everyone is an opportunity to touch the sacred. Nothing is too obscure or grandiose for God. But we must develop the eyes to see.

As you sort through the raw material of your life, trust that you are looking at something sacred. You are looking at God's creative presence, the story of you. This raw material points to your utter uniqueness and provides insight into what you mean to the world. That Divine Spark is the energy pulsing through seemingly mundane moments. If you sit with the mundane, if you allow these little moments time to speak to you, you will begin to see the larger story at work. You will begin to see the patterns in your life, where God is calling you from and what God is calling you for. You will see the stories God has written into your very self and into the people around you.

Our stories reveal something unique and precious about ourselves, but they do so within a particular community, a group, a society. Human beings are not simply dropped into the world; we're formed. That's why the power of storytelling lies in its ability to connect—and why it's important to remember that a spirituality of storytelling connects us not only with others, but with our deepest selves and with God.

As Pope Francis says: "It is not a matter of simply telling stories as such, or of advertising ourselves, but rather of remembering who and what we are in God's eyes, bearing witness to what the Spirit writes in our hearts and revealing to everyone that his or her story contains marvelous things."[1]

Christians believe that we are made in the image and likeness of God. God is the great storyteller, the Creator who made the entirety of the universe—all that we see and dare imagine. We are made in the image and likeness, then, of this great storyteller. We are called to create through our stories, to usher in something new and wonderful, to discover the role we play in the great story of the universe. We discover that God is in all things, in all stories, in each of us.

— PART 1 —

WHO AM I?

Someone had forgotten to turn on the air conditioning. Against the heat of August in Baltimore in an old Catholic church, that was fast becoming a problem.

I leaned over to my brother—my best man—and said, "If I give the signal, you need to find Alli a bottle of water." He gulped and nodded. I could see the sweat forming beneath the beautiful wedding dress. I watched the Jesuit priest wipe his forehead. There was more than a bit of sweat dripping down my own.

Weddings, as anyone who's planned one can attest, are just as much about the guests as they are about the couple. And I was sitting at the front of the church, sandwiched between my bride and my brother, staring out at our hundred or so guests, and I was worried. This was a full Catholic Mass, and we'd barely scratched the First Reading. People were already restless, and I didn't want this moment of prayer—of coming together before God and community—to be forgotten amid sweat and heat and discomfort. The readings, the prayers, the people, and the symbols we'd so carefully chosen to kick-start our married life were suddenly looking more and more like obstacles to a glass of cold water.

All we could do was hope that big old Saint Ignatius Church, with its sputtering HVAC system, would soon be just a bit cooler.

A disaster? No. We laugh about it now. And in fact, those readings, those prayers we'd selected with such intentionality, won the day. What we were trying to say to our family and friends—what we were trying to say to each other—came through. And the Holy Spirit hovered in the room.

Toward the end of the ceremony, my brother and sister-in-law—the best man and maid of honor, respectively—climbed the podium to read what is commonly referred to as the Arrupe Prayer. (We'll put aside the fact that the late superior general of the Jesuits, Pedro Arrupe, did not write it.)

"Nothing is more practical than finding God, than falling in Love in a quite absolute, final way," my brother began. "What you are in love with, what seizes your imagination, will affect everything."

"It will decide what will get you out of bed in the morning," continued my sister-in-law. "What you do with your evenings, how you spend your weekends, what you read, whom you know, what breaks your heart, and what amazes you with joy and gratitude." Together they concluded: "Fall in Love, stay in love, and it will decide everything."

This prayer isn't just for those celebrating their marriage vows. This is a prayer of discernment, of vocation, of discovering those hopes and dreams, passions and insights, that the Holy Spirit has placed within you. In uncovering those things—in uncovering *what will get you out of bed in the morning*—you begin to recognize what matters most to you, those things you value.

We simply cannot answer the question *Who am I?* without digging deeply into our values. And failing to answer this question brings our Ignatian storytelling to a sudden stop. How can we accept who we are if we haven't done the hard work of figuring it out? How can we heal our past wounds if we don't identify them in our story? Who we are, what we can contribute to the common good, our unique perspective on the needs of our world—all of this is instrumental to our own stories—and to accompanying others in telling theirs.

The stories that contribute to our understanding of self and our place in the world depend on our knowing what we value and what we stand for. If we don't take values seriously—ours and others'—then we cannot drive effective action, from simple things like buying groceries to more complex things like raising children. To riff on that wedding prayer, we remain in bed all day because we never figured out what gets us up in the morning.

In this book's first part, we dig into who we are and what makes us tick. To do so, we develop three Ignatian storytelling practices:

- **We exercise our imagination** by encountering God in Scripture. We place ourselves in those well-worn stories and seek to discover something new about ourselves and our world. Cultivating this Ignatian imagination reveals what we hold most important by placing us in the context of God's own stories.

- **We employ the *examen*,** that time-tested prayer of the Jesuits, to help us look back over our own life story. We sink deep into the mundane nitty-grittiness of daily life, looking for God at work in the patterns of our days. The *examen* helps us articulate those things we hold dear so as to better express them to others.

- Finally, **we reflect on cannonball moments,** those big moments of conversion that are reflective of Ignatius's own life story. Shifting away from the nitty-gritty, we look to the life-altering: those moments in our stories that challenge us to reassess our values, to let them grow or cast them aside.

In this first part of our journey together, know that you are a beloved child of God. Your hurts are God's hurts; your joys are God's joys. And everything in between? God's there, too.

— 1 —

When Values and Actions Don't Match

Ignatian spirituality is built on a rather stunning premise: God of the universe desires to deal directly with us, God's beloved creations. God desires to sink deep into our stories—the mess of it all, the highs and lows and embarrassments—and take a long, loving look at what makes us tick. In fact, discovering what is important to us, what we profess to believe and value, is pivotal to understanding and accepting who we are. Naming those values and bringing them before God, realizing that it was God who put them there in the first place, is where we begin our journey in Ignatian storytelling. God created good things in creating each of us. Recognizing and claiming those values that guide us is key to recognizing and claiming our own goodness.

You are the main character of your story. And as you know from reading and watching countless stories, a character's motivation leads that character to make certain decisions and take certain actions. Your motivation springs from your values, what is important to you. So, without a firm understanding of what you value and of how those values lead you to action, your life—your story—might sputter and stall.

In this chapter, I invite you to reflect on your values. What are they? What do they point to? How do they guide your life? As you recognize those things that are important, you'll begin to see how they impact daily life, or where they fail to do so. Too often, what we think we value isn't actually translating into everyday activities. This misalignment between who we are and who we'd like to be is taxing on our spirit. As a result, we feel as though we're letting down ourselves and those around us. But it doesn't have to be that way.

• • •

"Do you have any change?"

We've all heard those words, I'm sure, on sidewalks and street corners and outside busy marketplaces. Someone looking to us for a little help. How do we respond? With charity? Generosity? Or suspicion? Most important, how do we *want* to respond? How do we think we *should*?

I was new to the city of Baltimore, renting a room on the third floor of a classic Baltimore-style rowhome in the Charles Village neighborhood, about three miles north of downtown. I had moved to the city to start a job at Catholic Relief Services. I was to be the newest member of the team that develops the annual Lenten faith-in-action program, CRS Rice Bowl.

Despite growing up in the suburbs north of Philadelphia, I'd been to Baltimore only once or twice. I was very much *not* a city dweller. My understanding of my new hometown was a hodgepodge of facts revolving around crime and the aquarium and what I could glimpse from I-95 when en route to Washington, DC.

So it was no surprise that when two friends—fellow former volunteers from a Salesian mission program serving in Santa Cruz, Bolivia—came to visit me, I knew very little about the sights the city had to offer. I had one walking tour in my arsenal and proceeded to take my friends along that route. "Do you mind walking?" I asked, and they said no, and off we went. It was July in Baltimore, a hot day.

Our journey took us south of my place in Charles Village toward the Inner Harbor. We stopped for crepes just north of Penn Station, and that's where it happened: a scene now so etched into my mind, so pivotal in shaping my own forthcoming experiences of Baltimore, so common and mundane, that it was hardly noticeable to anyone but me.

The three of us approached the door, deciding that crepes would indeed be a delicious way to spend our lunch, and a man approached, down on his luck, likely without a permanent home, not unpleasant or rude. He had been lingering outside the small restaurant and, upon seeing us, set himself on a course that would collide with ours just in front of the door.

"Do you have any change?"

The question that I have grown nearly deaf to, the one that washes over me like icy water: uncomfortable for a few moments but forgotten within the hour. I lower my head and reach for the door. But my friends do not. Their heads are not lowered, their eyes not cast aside. They do not reach past the man but rather stop and greet him with a smile.

"Buddy," my one friend replied, "I don't carry any cash, but I'd be more than happy to buy you a crepe. Whichever one you'd like."

The man smiled, nodded, and said, "I'd like that. Thank you."

My other friend opened the door for him and ushered him inside, talking to him the whole time, asking his name, his story, where he lived. They bought him a savory crepe (certainly not the cheapest on the menu), and we waited with him as it was prepared.

And then, off he went, the whole encounter over in just a few minutes. I guess he liked the food, but I'll never know because he, like us, had other places to be.

Nothing revolutionary happened; every day, people buy food for those who are down on their luck. People stop and talk to those on the streets of Baltimore, New York, Philadelphia—every city in the world.

But I was dumbfounded. Embarrassed. Struck by the stark contrast between my knee-jerk reaction in front of the crepe shop and that of my friends. Encountering that man, responding in a way that didn't compute with my original intentions of purchasing a crepe and then continuing to the harbor—reverberated in my thoughts for the remainder of that day and beyond.

Not so for my companions. Their knee-jerk reaction was one of love, compassion, and fellowship. There was nothing further to think on; they did what they believed to be right. Their actions perfectly manifested what they saw to be important, just, human. And that stuck with me.

How might I reach a point where that was *my* immediate response? Because I knew that it wasn't a matter of simply buying a crepe for everyone I met on the streets. It was a matter of looking inward and challenging what I found there, digging deep to understand my own values, my sense of self, and where those values failed to manifest in the actions of my daily life.

As we endeavor to make sense of our own stories, as we grapple with what they point to about ourselves and our place in the world, a key component is articulating our values in a way that is clear, inviting, and actionable. Ignatian storytelling hinges on it.

What Made Jesus So Attractive?

Do you ever wonder if this is what drew people to Jesus? It's so easy for us to grow jaded reading the Gospels; what did Jesus *really* say that convinced people to utterly uproot their lives? Were they so unhappy that *anything* was better? I can't believe that; otherwise my faith is simply one of desperation. Did they really grasp the theological implications of Jesus' preaching? I have a hard time believing that, too, because, more often than not, we see the apostles confused by Jesus' explanation, missing the point entirely. In fact, we see that same confusion today. It seems a far cry to claim that it was solely Jesus' teaching that drew the crowds.

I have to think that what first and foremost drew people to Jesus was what he *did* and who he *was*. His knee-jerk reaction was one of love; he stopped and talked with those standing outside the crepe shop. He ushered them inside and bought them a savory crepe. And people like me stood and watched, our mouths agape because that was never what we were going to do, not in a million years.

But now, seeing it done with such love and joy, seeing it done so *naturally*—maybe that kind of instinct was achievable. Maybe it was worth hanging around people who didn't avert their eyes from a person in need, who met and held their gaze and then acted. And the person who managed to do just that—well, I might just follow that guy to see what comes next. See if he has any fishes, loaves or, better yet, wine to multiply.

What to do with all this? For me, as a Catholic Christian, the person of Jesus Christ is central to my faith. His is the standard against which I examine my life and actions; his is the standard from which so many of my values flow. That might be true for you, too. But you might also have in mind a different spiritual figure, someone to whom you look for inspiration and encouragement, someone after whom you model your life. The values we hold are often passed down to us through our families, communities, churches, and schools.

For Saint Ignatius of Loyola and for the spirituality that bears his name, Jesus is central. An encounter with Jesus is one important way in which Ignatius encourages each of us to better understand ourselves. But that encounter isn't an academic exercise; Ignatius doesn't say we should simply study the stories of Scripture. Rather, to examine ourselves, we need to place ourselves alongside Jesus. This is a form of prayer and a way of reading Scripture that depends on our imagination. And it is through our imagination that God helps us better understand our stories: what we've been given, why it matters, and what we have to contribute.

Meeting Jesus through the Imagination

Imagination was significant for Ignatius. He didn't simply read the words of Scripture; he imagined the scene. If Jesus and his followers were walking through the streets of Jerusalem, Ignatius heard the sounds of the busy marketplace and smelled the food cooking at the nearest stall. He felt the sand on his exposed skin and the sweat from the day's heat. He interrogated his emotions when Jesus spoke: Did these words bring him comfort? Did they challenge him? Was he upset or motivated to act? Why?

Ignatius had an idea of who he was and wanted to be. But by allowing himself this degree of honesty and vulnerability before God through the stories of Scripture, Ignatius began to see where he fell short and where God was inviting him to something new.

From this intense experience of prayer, this deep immersion in the stories of Scripture, Ignatius emerged better able to meet the needs of *his* story as it played out in his particular time and place. What was Jesus asking of him *today*? How was the comfort or discomfort he felt studying at Jesus' feet meant to inform how he responded to Jesus present in the people *currently* around him? The inner stirrings that these encounters with Jesus evoked helped Ignatius identify what was really important to him: the values that would guide his life and work.

This type of prayer can be intense, even uncomfortable. It can reveal things about ourselves that we prefer to remain hidden. But if we seek healing through our stories, we must accept who we *really* are, not who we'd like to be or pretend to be on Instagram. Our work begins there.

When I was younger and would listen to the stories of Jesus, I would often be shocked at the inaction of the people in the Gospel narratives. I would find myself drawn to Simon, who helps Jesus carry the cross, or to Joseph of Arimathea, who, though late in the game, helps by offering his tomb to bury Jesus' body. My second-grade mind would identify with these seeming heroes, though not without casting just a touch of judgment their way. After all, Simon is *pressed* into service; Joseph was a disciple in *secret*.

But those others, my younger self had little patience for: those throngs of people gathered outside Pilate's window only to condemn Jesus by their silence. What of the many who watched as Jesus struggled on his way to Calvary? How could they *not* stand up to defend him? It was *Jesus*. Didn't they *know* eternal life hung in the balance? Didn't these people *get it*?

All these years later, it's easy to say that *I* was the one who didn't get it. Or perhaps I did; perhaps that was the mind of a child at work, simply and easily navigating between what was good and right and what was wrong and shameful. But it was the mind of a child with privilege, who had not encountered so much of the world: racism, sexism, homophobia, xenophobia, poverty, oppression, and violence. For me, then, Jesus was simply a man who had lived more than two thousand years ago; he was hardly the Christ that we encounter every day in faces so different and yet sharing in that common thread of human dignity.

Of *course* I would stand up for *Jesus*, but that guy on the street who spits as he talks, who smells of smoke and garbage, whose clothes are stained: I imagine he's someone else's problem. Or those images of communities in countries near and far, where food and water are daily struggles—man, I *wish* someone would help them. And what about the Black and Brown bodies—bodies just like Jesus'—crushed under systems of racism and oppression? I mean, that's bad, but is it something that I need to worry about?

And over the years, I've met with an uncomfortable truth. I wouldn't have stood up for Jesus. I would have remained quiet in the crowd. I would have been a passive onlooker, upset, maybe irked at the injustice of it all, but silent nonetheless. Perhaps even judging Jesus: He should have *known* he was getting himself into trouble. Judging those Jesus stood with: that person *did* break the law, so *shouldn't* we stone her?

As I visit those scenes in my prayer again and again—the road to Calvary, the crowd before Pilate, even moments with the apostles as they encounter the crippled, the blind, the sick—I find that so often *I* am the one paralyzed by resentment, fear, and inaction. I, too, cry out, "Crucify him," though not in so many words. And it is a humbling, frightening thought.

This is why we place ourselves alongside Jesus in Scripture: to see how we react. To understand who God is calling us to be and to uncover those obstacles in ourselves that prevent us from fully becoming that person.

Ultimately, Ignatius's imaginative prayer is an exercise in discovering where our values fail to align with the values of Christ. We all project versions of ourselves, not unlike what my second-grade self did. We all see ourselves as the heroes of the story.

But when push comes to shove, do we live out those values? Do those values drive action? Or do we fall silent in the crowd?

An Exercise in Ignatian Storytelling

Opening Prayer

Pray for the grace to identify the values that underpin your life and to uncover where you fall short of acting on them.

Prayer Text

Now someone approached him and said, "Teacher, what good must I do to gain eternal life?" He answered him, "Why do you ask me about the good? There is only One who is good. If you wish to enter into life, keep the commandments." He asked him, "Which ones?" And Jesus replied, "'You shall not kill; you shall not commit adultery; you shall not steal; you shall not bear false witness; honor your father and your mother'; and 'you shall love your neighbor as yourself.'" The young man said to him, "All of these I have observed. What do I still lack?" Jesus said to him, "If you wish to be perfect, go, sell what you have and give to [the] poor, and you will have treasure in heaven. Then come, follow me." When the young man heard this statement, he went away sad, for he had many possessions. Then Jesus said to his disciples, "Amen, I say to you, it will be hard for one who is rich to enter the kingdom of heaven." (Matthew 19:16–23)

Reflection Exercise

- Recall an instance when you lived out your values. What values did you manifest? Why? How did your values impact the lives of those around you?
- Recall an instance when your values were challenged. Did you stand by what you believed? Were you made better by this challenge? Did your values come into deeper clarity?

Conversation

Choose one of the instances identified above. Then read the prayer text. Imagine yourself discussing this instance with Jesus. Do you align with Jesus' values and vision for the world, or do you find yourself walking away? How does this make you feel? Talk to Jesus about this.

Journal

- What do you value? What are your values? Where do they come from?
- Do your values align with those of Jesus? Why, or why not? How might you recalibrate them?

— 2 —

The Storytelling Practice of Hope

It's tempting to think that we are alone in our good work. Even if we discover and claim our values, we might be tempted to keep them hidden, thinking that only we hold these things to be important.

But Ignatius's approach to prayer, his desire to understand what God was asking of him in the present moment, reflects his recognition of God's story as *the* story of humanity: There was a direct thread from Jesus' time to Ignatius's. Lessons and insights echoed down through the ages; this was the same story. Ignatius was meant to grapple with the needs of his moment just as Jesus grappled with the needs of *his* moment and as countless communities of saints and sinners grappled with the needs of their moments before his time and after.

Why? Because in this great story of God's people, what we see are themes that resonate across the human experience: friendship, compassion, mercy, love, suffering, hope, redemption, and resurrection. These aren't merely things that we know to be true in the human experience; they are values we seek. They're values we desire to bring to others and to call forth from others. They're values we look to in order to create common cause and promote the common good.

And values are important because what we value in life, what we deem important and worth struggling for, dictates how we spend our days, our money, our time with friends and family: what gets us out of bed in the morning.

If you've discovered something that you value, that directs and inspires you in your daily activities, isn't it likely that others have done the same? Isn't it likely that what you value might mirror what others value, too? And if so, how might you share that experience? Amplifying your own values to reach through your story to the stories of others invites not just individual healing but also the healing of communities.

Through the Stories of Others

I was glad I'd packed boots; though, to be honest, one wrong step, and I would have sunk well past my waist into the muck of the rice paddies.

I was in Vietnam documenting the humanitarian and development work of Catholic Relief Services. My colleagues and I were spending the week with the Phan family, who lived just outside of Hoi An. (I've changed their name for privacy.) The juxtaposition was harsh: Hoi An is a coastal tourist town, known for its old-city charm and array of restaurants and shops. It's safe and prosperous and easy to pop in and out of as an outsider and feel as though you've experienced something of authentic Vietnam.

The Phans lived about twenty minutes by car from our hotel. And their neighborhood was far from touristy. Their home was a simple, one-floor cement structure: two bedrooms, a small living space, and a kitchen. They had erected a few other makeshift structures to house the pig and the cow and the chickens and the huge pot in which they cooked most of their meals. A few of their neighbors lived in much larger, much more elaborate homes—an odd contrast in this otherwise struggling farm community—but most shared the Phans' simple lifestyle.

That lifestyle was a hard one. The rice paddies were their primary source of income, supplemented by what the cows, chickens, and pigs could produce. Of course, relying on one crop to make a living is a risky business, particularly when your competition is literally everyone in your neighborhood. The fact that increasingly frequent and dangerous storms could completely wipe out your livelihood—the fields, the livestock, and even your house, washed away and lost in a moment—kept these communities on the edge of poverty. The edge, in general.

So, we were traipsing through the rice paddies looking for snails. It was hot and wet and uncomfortable. Snails, as I would learn, were another source of income. And protein. And for the Phan family and their neighbors, protein was in short supply. Good nutrition was in short supply. In fact, their two eldest sons were stunted, never to reach their full physical, mental, and economic potential because they hadn't received the nutrition they needed at a young age. They would never fully develop. As we wandered up and down the dusty street, we observed that their story was not uncommon. Their story, in fact, is all too common in countries around the world.

No number of snails would fix that.

And yet, Mr. and Mrs. Phan set out each and every day, and often at night, too, to dig those slimy critters out of the muck. Hours spent under the hot Vietnamese sun meticulously combing through the paddies. Returning empty-handed to the old motorcycle, rolling along to the next field, the next snail-hunting ground, in the hope their neighbors hadn't already depleted the stock.

And then back home, where the whole family would wash and pack the snails, bundle them up and weigh them, to be sold to a buyer from the city. Mrs. Phan would sit with her neighbors, bag of snails in hand—a bag that looked identical to that of her neighbors, her friends—and they'd all get just a bit of money for their hours of hard labor. No haggling, just acceptance of what the buyer offered.

I couldn't do it. In the sun and heat, holding tightly to my camera, I could barely keep up. It was so hot, so steamy, that each morning when we arrived at the house, we'd wait twenty minutes just for our camera lenses to adjust to the heat; they became impossibly foggy the moment they interacted with the day's humidity. I peeled off layers of sweat-ridden clothes each evening, desperate for a shower. And I drank water like—well, because—my life depended on it.

And so, later in the week, when we learned that Mrs. Phan didn't feel well, had been sick in the night, of course I said take it easy. How could she not feel ill? So much sun, heat, and hard labor. We can film you getting snails tomorrow, I said.

But, of course, that wasn't the primary worry. Mrs. Phan was 50 percent of the family's workforce; her husband couldn't possibly collect as many snails without her. This wasn't about the stories I was there to write; it was about their livelihood.

We still gave her the day off, at least from the pressure of our camera lenses. But she certainly didn't relax. She didn't get sick leave.

The True Test of Our Values

My encounter with the Phans was value-driven: I believed there was some good that could be done to support a vulnerable family and community, to educate young people, and to care for the environment. But the experience was an overwhelming one, and my belief in my ability, and in the ability of the people I represented, to make any difference at all swung back and forth between hope and despair, between values and a lack of self-worth.

It is often easy to identify our values in the abstract, in a vacuum, to examine them one at a time and imagine how we would live them out. The relevant value would flash above our heads in neon lights, and we'd do the slow work of demonstrating why it was important and how it impacted our daily decisions.

But that's not quite how these things work. We find ourselves in moments and situations that overwhelm us, in which our values are consumed by a fight-or-flight instinct. Everything collides, and we feel as though all we can do is remain standing. What's the value at stake here? Who are we called to be in this moment? Rather than recognize how we want to live, what drives us, and how that driving force might connect us to other people, we get trapped in self-isolation and despair.

A pernicious lie whispers in our ear: You have nothing to contribute to this moment. You have nothing of value in yourself. Just sit this one out.

Of course, that lie is not of God. And our stories are not built on lies.

I remember driving between the Phans' home and our hotel and thinking, *What is the story here?* Certainly there were plenty of compelling, visual details. A family wades through rice paddies to collect snails to supplement both income and nutrition. Farmers pool resources to maintain livelihoods in the face of a changing, devastating climate. Parents shackled by poverty still push their daughters to get an education.

None of these things was untrue. Each held a nugget of a story.

But the story I was there to find—the story I was tasked to bring back—was a story of hope. CRS' Lenten program is built upon these stories of hope. They're invitations to families across the United States to enter into solidarity with families around the world through the practices of prayer, fasting, and almsgiving. And while it's tempting to lean into the more dire aspects of individuals' stories—the unimaginable hunger, the constant anxiety over where the next meal will come from, the uncertainly over education, shelter, and security—these more sensational details serve only to distance the reader from the real people these stories are about.

That kind of hunger sounds awful. Here's a few bucks. I'm going to turn the page.

I can't even imagine living like that. It's too awful. What else can I find on YouTube?

This way of life is too far removed from mine. We have nothing in common. This is someone else's problem.

These kinds of emotions are action inhibitors.[2] Fear leads to paralysis: I'm overwhelmed and can't think of any action worth taking. Apathy or self-doubt becomes a self-fulfilling prophecy. Stories that make us feel isolated or removed from the needs at hand create walls between us and needed action. We just can't find common ground with the people in these stories. The temptation to tell an extreme story, one of the *direst* examples of poverty, violence, or oppression, can distort the reader's understanding of reality, leading readers to assume there might be no hope left; it's too late.

The antidote lies in action motivators: emotions like urgency, righteous anger, solidarity, and hope. "Because emotions are the medium through which we experience value, they provide us with vital information about the way we ought to live our lives as well as the motivation to live them in that way."[3] Stories that connect us to others, that pull us out of ourselves and remind us that we can make a meaningful difference, and do so now, are the kinds of stories that build a world in which all families can thrive and prosper. We resist romanticizing hope; we live in the harsh reality of the present. And yet we do so by pointing to concrete ways in which hope is made real and a real difference is made.

The Discipline to Hope

These are the kinds of stories that help us heal. We empower the subject of the story and the recipient of the story. Together, we declare that it's not too late.

It comes back to values. What do we believe is important? Which of our values are at stake in these stories, in this moment? How do those values intersect and align with those of others? And what do they demand of us?

The story I landed on for the Phan family centered on their eldest daughter. She struggled in all the ways her family did. But her story illustrated hope in several concrete ways. Here is a young girl who works alongside her family, who values her family, who cares for her parents when they fall ill, who goes to school each day, every afternoon, and who makes time for extra tutoring in the mornings. Her story is one of dreams, of determination, of resilience. Those values are embedded in her family, from the difficult decisions her parents have made.

We all want our children to succeed. We want the next generation to build great things, to thrive, to care for their elders. We identify with parents who make hard decisions. And we can begin to glimpse a path forward, a path out of the poverty that has entrapped so many, by empowering young women through education and job opportunities.

It takes discipline to tell a story of hope. Stories that dwell only on suffering, trauma, and chaos lead to more online clicks, more comments, and more division. But they may not lead to meaningful action. They may not help anyone heal.

This isn't a story about snails. It's not a story about the long hours spent mucking through the rice paddies. It's not a story about the coins those snails earn. This is a story of what the snails point to: a slow, steady, difficult-yet-determined march to full and flourishing humanity. The Phans' story reminds us that we all find ourselves in the muck collecting snails sometimes, and sometimes we need someone to help us climb out, which is okay. Such struggle is the work of life.

The values we weave into our stories and the emotions we stir in our listeners and ourselves can lead to action or stagnation. As Ignatian storytellers, we might frame this differently: there are values that help us heal, and then there are values that repel us from the needs of others and blind us to our own needs. We stare only at our perceived insufficiency, our inability to make a difference, either in our lives or in the lives of others. We end up justifying ourselves in averting our gaze from the needs of others, just as I justified avoiding the eyes of that man outside the crepe store.

Values that repel us from our common humanity, our shared world, trap us where we are. We get stuck in the muck as though we've stepped off the path in a Vietnamese rice field. There is no action to be taken; it's too late and hopeless.

But this is not the story God tells us.

When we walk with Jesus through the Scriptures, what do we see? What do we hear? What do we feel? Jesus is full of second chances, third chances, seventy-seventh chances. Even the final act of desolation, death itself, becomes a springboard to something new: the Resurrection. But in our lives, it's easy and tempting to dwell in the valley of death.

Many years ago when I was an undergraduate, a Jesuit priest and professor of film studies was reviewing a creative writing project of mine. I told him I was stuck. I couldn't think of a good story, a good ending. He said to me, "Why not tell an Easter story?" I didn't understand what he meant. None of my characters was dying; certainly, none of them was rising from the dead.

"It's the hope," he said. "It's what the story points to. What it inspires from within and without."

An Easter story doesn't necessarily tell of a protagonist dying and rising from the dead. It's a story in which the protagonist experiences transformation. One such transformation happens when the protagonist discovers what he or she holds most dear—those values that are at the root of their identity—and how they produce real, positive change.

We're invited into this Easter story. We're invited to discover what lies within the open tomb, what goodness God has placed within us and how it might guide us. And in so doing, we learn not only who we are but also how we might make a meaningful difference in the world by being simply who we've been created to be.

An Exercise in Ignatian Storytelling

Opening Prayer

Pray for the grace to identify how your values may better serve others.

Prayer Text

When the Pharisees heard that [Jesus] had silenced the Sadducees, they gathered together, and one of them [a scholar of the law] tested him by asking, "Teacher, which commandment in the law is the greatest?" He said to him, "You shall love the Lord, your God, with all your heart, with all your soul, and with all your mind. This is the greatest and the first commandment. The second is like it: You shall love your neighbor as yourself. The whole law and the prophets depend on these two commandments." (Matthew 22:34–40)

Reflection Exercise

- Consider how your sense of self-worth leads you to value the worth of others. How do your values guide you in this effort? Does this lead you to hope?
- Recall an instance when your values aligned with those of others. How did this moment of solidarity make you feel? Did it point to a more hopeful future?

Conversation

Talk to Jesus about how you desire to be perceived by others. Then talk about how your self-perception leads you to perceive others. Ask Jesus how he perceives you and those around you. Do you value yourself and others as Jesus does?

Journal

- What needs to change in how you view yourself and the world so that you might better align with Jesus?
- How do you practice hope in the stories you tell of yourself and others?

— 3 —

God Is in the Details

We've been told that the devil is in the details. From passing legislation to organizing school projects to getting new initiatives at work off the ground to simply painting the spare bedroom, the devil in the details is meant as a warning: If you delve too deeply into the nitty-gritty of logistics and next steps and consensus building, you'll inevitably run up against a roadblock. Thinking up big ideas is easy; actualizing them is hard. And we attribute that challenge to the devil in the details.

Let's turn that phrase around: It's God in the details, that same God who desires to sink deeply into who we are, what we love and value, and who we want to be. God isn't interested only in the broad strokes of our lives but also in the tiny, mundane moments. And for good reason. We spend a lot more time in these ordinary moments than we do in big, adventurous, blockbuster action. Our lives are the sum of so many quiet moments; we might call those mundane moments the building blocks of who we are and what we love.

The details, though, do reveal hardship too, as they did in the story of the Phan family. If I hadn't spent time focusing on the smaller moments that I spent in the Vietnamese countryside, I would have missed the feelings that welled up in me. Despite the challenges I faced—and the challenges I witnessed others facing—in allowing these moments to wash over me, I learned something about myself and the story I was there to witness.

This chapter is about details, about recognizing that although we may feel as if it's the devil we're encountering in those details, we're really experiencing the ebb and flow of God's Spirit. And Saint Ignatius gave us a tool to help us sink deeply into the Spirit at work in these quiet moments of a life story: the *examen*.

The Importance of Paying Attention

Our hedgehog went to church only once.

As it turns out, that's the same number of times she was spotted at a brewery. Or, not spotted, really. Hoosier was burrowed at the bottom of a bag, and we kept her there because it was a hot summer day, and she couldn't stay in the car. No one was ever the wiser, and, I assume, she learned a lot about beer.

On the day Hoosier went to church, it was the Feast of Saint Francis of Assisi. My wife was pregnant with our first child, and we had recently moved to a neighborhood in the northern part of Baltimore. We thought we'd check out the local Catholic community. It was only a few blocks from our house, and who didn't like a nice autumn walk?

We attended Mass there for just a few months, but those weeks happened to fall over the Feast of Saint Francis, October 4, and, as is tradition, the pastor promised to bless the animals. Hoosier, our hedgehog, could use all the blessings she could get. Winter was coming, and hedgehogs are notorious for courting death during the colder months. At least mine was, attempting to hibernate when really all she was doing was shutting down her vital organs.

"I remember when we got Max blessed," I said to my wife as we wrapped Hoosier in blankets and old T-shirts and stuck her in her travel bag. "The only ferret the priest had ever seen."

She nodded and rolled her eyes and reminded me that she had heard that story before.

We trudged back up the hill, through the crisp autumn air, back to the church, hedgehog in tow. We looked somewhat lost as we carried our bundle of spikes and quills and sniffing sounds through the suspiciously empty parking lot.

"Where is everyone?" my wife asked. "Did we miss it?"

"We couldn't have missed it," I replied. "It started at one." It was, at that point, about one thirty. And it seemed far-fetched, in my mind, that a solitary priest could administer the blessing of the Lord to what I assumed was an ark full of cats, dogs, birds, and small mammals. The scene in my mind was akin to a PetSmart, only instead of purchasing dog food and litter, the clientele was purchasing assurances that all dogs do indeed go to heaven.

"You guys here for the blessing?" A single voice. The gardener, it seemed, working on the landscaping. *Just like in Scripture*, I thought. *Jesus himself has come to bless our hedgehog.*

"We are," I confirmed.

The man nodded. "What you got there?"

"A hedgehog."

"A hedgehog?"

"A hedgehog."

"Never seen one of those."

No one ever had. In fact, quite frequently, people tried to convince us that what we had was a porcupine, which is one of the deadliest creatures in the world.

"I'll show you," I said, already unwrapping Hoosier.

"Nah, that's alright," the man replied. "I'll go get Father. Go up and around."

We found ourselves at the rectory door. And in the two minutes it took us to reach that point, a dozen or so people appeared, seemingly out of the landscape itself, whispering among themselves that these two folks had shown up with a pet hedgehog.

I say with all kindness that this moment felt a bit horror-movie-esque. Strangers, old and young, converge on my wife, myself, and our hedgehog from all sides, materializing out of nothing, whispering about us amongst themselves as though we weren't there and very much within earshot. Mumbling, eyes darting, they surrounded us. The word *blessing* was spoken by a few of them.

And then from behind us—this is not an exaggeration—the door to the rectory bursts open and the pastor, a big man with a burly white beard, appears, sleeves rolled up as if he's been hanging drapes, collar simply missing, and he bellows: "Are you the ones with the hedgehog?"

Yes, we say, and he ushers us closer, produces a stole out of thin air, and holy water, too. "Let us all offer a prayer for this hedgehog, for—what's its name?" A questioning eyebrow raised.

"Hoosier."

And then, all these horror-movie extras are suddenly in a circle around us, hands extended, as Father says some words that I imagine were a blessing though they're lost to the sands of time. The moment is more of a still image in my memory than a clip with audio.

And just like that, he smiles, closes the door, and the crowd disperses. Like there was never anyone else even there. And the two of us, and Hoosier, are standing alone, stunned.

"What just happened?" my wife asked.

I shrugged. "I think we got our blessing."

And it must have stuck, too, because Hoosier went on to live six and a half years, which is pretty good if you're a hedgehog.

• • •

The random specificity of this story is the point. It's detailed and specific and, maybe, interesting, but at the end of it, you might have shrugged. This guy's got a thing for small animals, you may have said, grasping for a theme, a moral. Who cares? What an odd anecdote.

My creative writing professors emphasized again and again, Be specific. Drop your readers into the scene and let them look around. Let them *feel* what's going on. It's the difference between your protagonist walking by some trash and your protagonist passing by an old Coca-Cola can that had fallen from the bin and was now the temporary shelter for a whole family of industrious ants.

That level of detail is important in a story. Those details pull at you, bring you back into the story, alongside the characters, and demand a second look. Your listener or reader gets inundated with facts and names and places, but if you hook them with one, key detail, something vivid and personal, they won't forget it. That detail can become an entry point into whatever larger message you're trying to convey.

It's the purple flower in a little girl's hair. It's the perpetually unlaced shoe on a teen's left foot. It's the lopsided grin that refuses to sag in the face of impossible odds. Maybe it's even the holy hedgehog.

Jesus himself told us to be on the lookout for these kinds of details. Not in so many words, perhaps, but think for a moment on the Lord's Prayer. The line that sticks with me is this: Give us *this* day our *daily* bread. There is a recognition that there is something particular in this day, in this moment, that demands the attention of the divine, for which we need to be on the lookout. Some need to be met, some challenge to be overcome, some small detail that will serve as an entry point into a larger mission. Think over your day: What detail immediately jumps to mind? What image or word or scent or sound? What does it stir in you?

Let's return to the *examen*, that simple prayer that Saint Ignatius left us with as a tool for looking back at these moments of daily bread. It goes like this: Recognize the presence of the Spirit, express gratitude for the ongoing gift and gifts of life, and mull over the day—the good, the bad, the random—with God. Specificity is key, because in pondering specific moments of the day through the eyes of God, we have the potential to glimpse something greater, to see God at work in the minutiae, in ways we likely missed. Our prayer over time reveals patterns of God at work in our lives, opportunities and invitations from God to apply skills and experiences and passions. Over the course of our *examen*, we commit to improving ourselves, to making up for those failings—perhaps, mistakes we made without even realizing it—and to reconciling relationships.

It all comes down to the details. To little silly stories about hedgehogs and blessings and ordinary autumn days. Because God is present in and through it all, there isn't a moment in daily life that isn't threaded by the divine. And so, being attentive to these details, these ordinary happenings, helps us understand where God is at work and how God is at work *in us*. In this way we are reminded that God is present every moment and that God cares deeply for each of us, God's beloved creatures.

Even if we struggle to see the meaning in our stories, we can at least take comfort in knowing that the God of the universe believes our stories are worth paying attention to. Slowly, then, we accept that maybe there's something more to our stories than we first thought, that these seemingly unimportant details actually mean something. We matter, and so does the *stuff* of our lives.

This is precisely how we stumble upon and how we recognize and form and nurture those important values we discussed in the last chapter.

God Is in the Details

I can remember my grandfather reading the newspaper. He would sit at the near end of the kitchen table in my grandparents' home, one foot in the kitchen, one foot in the living room, the sections sprawled out in front of him. I remember that because he would always ask me if I had read the paper that day, and if so, what I had learned.

I had never read the paper on the day in question. Or, any day, given that I was ten years old.

No matter. I'd earn myself a deep frown—wrinkles accented his forehead, nose scrunched up, lips pursed together—and a not-so-gentle reminder that I needed to know what was going on in the world. Then, he'd return to his perusal, calling out interesting headlines now and again to my grandmother, until he settled on an in-depth review of the local grocery store sales.

"Dolly," he'd say to my grandmother. "Watermelon's on sale this week."

"Dolly," he'd call. "Buy-one-get-one can of black beans."

"Dolly," he'd yell. "Here's a good coupon for meat loaf."

We always joked that my grandparents' basement was like a fallout shelter; there were so many jars of tomato sauce and cans of beans that when COVID-19 struck in 2020, one of the things we *didn't* worry about was whether or not my grandparents had enough food. All those sales were finally paying dividends.

The price of food was a frequent topic of conversation around my grandparents' kitchen table. We'd arrive, sit down, exchange the normal check-ins on health and schooling, and then launch into how much cabbage was that week.

"How much they charging down by you?" my grandfather would ask my mom. Her response would elicit either a scoff of disapproval—"You're paying too much!"—or eyes full of wonder at the deals yet to arrive in Phillipsburg.

To an outsider, this sounds ludicrous. And if family legend is true, in the early days, my dad was a bit confused himself at the constant talk of grocery-store prices, coming from a family where politics was the kitchen table topic of choice.

But we weren't really talking about how much ham cost on Thursday. Those dizzying details were pointing to something much deeper: a history of immigrants, of a young couple who arrived in the United States from Syria, who raised five children in a narrow row home in Phillipsburg, New Jersey—the home they would both die in—who were proud to see their son, my grandfather, start a family of his own, who went off to war and came home with a wound he would never fully heal from, who would work long hours at a printing press to provide for his own family, to give them something better than he had, than his parents had, and ultimately, to smile proudly—from behind a wrinkled brow and weary eyes—at his grandchildren and great-grandchildren as they pursued lives beyond his wildest imagination. For my grandfather, all this was made possible by saving a few cents on ham every other Thursday.

Whenever I find myself in a conversation over a trivial thing like the price of ham, I think of my grandparents. Those kinds of conversations bring me great comfort. Though seemingly about nothing, to me they're about everything below the surface of dollars and cents and grocery-store items. These conversations speak to comfort and trust, mental relaxation, enjoyment of the present company. There is no need to raise your mental guard, to try to outdo your conversational sparring partner. You just settle in and rest in the presence of another person.

I tried to express as much to good friends of mine once. I was drawing a juxtaposition between the current conversation and a recent conversation I'd had with someone else over politics. I noted how I enjoyed the present company so much more because the conversation didn't demand such mental gymnastics.

My friends took this to mean I thought they were boring. An honest mistake. I had failed to express to them what these kinds of conversations represented to me, the true values at stake. I may not have been able to articulate it. Had they known that what I was really trying to say was that they reminded me of my grandparents, of family, of a warm and loving home and deep hospitality, I think they would have taken my bumbling remarks as one of the highest of compliments.

But they didn't. And the fault is mine because I wasn't able to properly express the values at the root of the story.

Do you recognize when values in your life manifest themselves? Are you able to put your finger on those moments and then point them out to others?

• • •

In the last chapter, we reflected on values as they relate to emotions, to feelings. We reflected on the difference between emotions that motivate us to act on those values and emotions that inhibit action. Exploring how and why emotions inspire values helps us to connect with others, to evoke in our listeners and readers similar emotions and thus open the door to shared values we can act upon together.

What I've tried to illustrate so far in this chapter is another important, complementary path to uncovering and sharing our values. Though it may seem that I've simply thrown a handful of story scraps at your feet, what I've tried to do is illustrate the many insignificant moments that, when woven together, create a tapestry of personal values. How do stories of hedgehog blessings and coupon-cutting grandfathers connect? Taken apart, they don't. But when woven together, we might begin to construct a narrative of family: a family being built upon meager savings, upon a shared faith, upon simple acts done together.

Leadership guru Simon Sinek gave one of the most popular TED Talks of all time. It's called "How Great Leaders Inspire Action." In it, he lays out a rather simple yet profound challenge: "People don't buy what you do, they buy why you do it. And what you do simply proves what you believe."[4] He encourages people to begin with *why*. Why start that new business? Why begin a new graduate program? Why get married? Why move to that city?

The easy answer, he notes, always highlights the *what*. "I'm starting a bakery." "I'm studying marketing." "I'm marrying my longtime partner." "I'm moving to Nashville." These answers don't get at the *why*. They give a very factual *what*.

To get at *why* is to get at values, beliefs, something deeper. "I'm starting this bakery business because I believe in creating opportunity in my community." "I'm beginning this graduate program because I think marketing can help me share ideas that I'm passionate about." "I'm getting married because I think together my partner and I are able to do good in the world." "I'm moving to Nashville because I want to be surrounded by music lovers." There are a dozen more *whys* to dig into in each of these answers, but you begin to see the difference.

When I returned from Vietnam and began sharing the stories of what I had witnessed, I told stories not of the high-tech, innovative, and frankly, groundbreaking climate technology that our teams were using to help farmers predict and respond to changing weather patterns. The machine was impressive, if, in appearance, a funny array of metallic tubes sitting in a rice paddy.

This machine was *what* we did. It was *how* we did it. But it wasn't *why* our work was important. The work mattered because young Vietnamese girls whose families had been terrorized by war in the past and typhoons in the present could now dream dreams about the future, dreams that included an education, a profession, and a life beyond poverty.

The truth was in the details: the girls' smiles, the backpacks they wore representing their days in school, the bike—their transportation—leaning against the cement house, the hard work they put into their chores.

And the connection was in the small details from my own life, details I know mirror the lives of others. Surely we all have a moment from our story of desperate daydreaming. Surely we all have an item from our past that represented our hoped-for future. Surely we all have foggy memories of a significant conversation that changed, if ever so slightly, the trajectory of our path.

As you reflect on your own day, you'll readily see the *what* of your story, a list of things you've done or are planning to do. Go deeper. Ask yourself *why*. Even something so simple as cleaning the bathroom. Why are you cleaning the bathroom? (I ask myself that question once a week.) Because you want a clean space? Because you want to make sure others feel comfortable in that space? Because you want to create a space that is welcoming, hospitable, comfortable?

It sounds like your weekly chore is actually a manifestation of an important value: hospitality. And that value is likely something you share with others.

These are the morsels of daily bread we pray over in the Lord's Prayer. We follow these bread crumbs; we follow where God is leading, knowing God walks with us. In so doing, we find ourselves in solidarity with others, recognizing, if opaquely, parallels in our stories, cracked windows through which we can climb in together. This is the very heart of the Ignatian *examen*.

Shared Values, Different Vocations

There was a shuttle operated by a local university that took students from the main campus to the medical campus every thirty minutes or so. I was not a student, but I did live along the route, and if I was able to get the shuttle, I could cut my commute significantly. So, for the first several months of my time at CRS, I rode to work with a bunch of future doctors, nurses, and other medical professionals. It was overwhelming.

I remember sitting in this quiet bus glancing over at my fellow passengers, clad in white jackets or blue scrubs, and feeling lost. Here were folks who were committed to helping people. They were often buried in imposing books. Snippets of conversation revealed high-stress, high-stakes situations. And here I was, riding to my job which, at best, involved sharing thirdhand stories from people on the other side of the world.

Man, if only I were doing the kind of good *these* people were doing.

Any temporary dream I had of becoming a doctor while riding that bus was quickly cut short by a reminder that my *own* blood made me queasy and that just talking about medical procedures made me somewhat light-headed.

I was not destined to be a doctor or a nurse. To be honest, I'd probably have a hard time simply sitting at the receptionist's desk at a pediatrician's office.

What I was experiencing, though, was important to reflect on. This was a shared value; the nurses on the bus, like me, cared about helping others, about building a better world. Our *why* was probably similar. Where we differed was the *how* and the *what*. And that's a good thing. Shared values acted upon through a variety of vocations build up society and the common good.

Details like these serve as bumpers on life's bowling alley. They keep us bouncing down the lane in the right direction, even if we're not always rolling quite as straight as we'd like. Naming these details again and again over time helps us recognize patterns where God is at work. The *examen* brings these patterns into focus.

As we sink into life's messy, seemingly random details, we piece together a larger narrative. Holy patterns emerge. We see that our passions and desires point to similar things—and have for some time. We discover that our skills, when applied judiciously, begin to yield results that build on one another. We find ourselves being called upon by our friends and families to respond to specific needs, to answer recurring questions. That is, if we have eyes to see.

In short, our role in our community, our purpose in life—dare we dream so big!—comes into some clarity. These small details and the feelings they evoke in us pull back the curtain on what is important, on what we value. Likely, they also reveal holes in our lives, places of emptiness and yearning.

• • •

God is in the details. But God doesn't force us to recognize that divine whisper. In fact, it's entirely possible to miss God's gentle nudge all together. If we don't pay attention, if we don't interrogate and organize and reorganize those details, we might never quite make sense of who God is inviting us to become. We might let our values wither on the vine, never fully grasping what gives them nourishment and deep roots, and without understanding what good work might come from them.

That's why that *examen* prayer is so important. That constant, muttered plea for daily bread. We look for big events to change us, to pick us up and drop us where we're meant to be. Those do happen, and we'll reflect on some in the next chapter. But most of life is lived in the ordinary.

An Exercise in Ignatian Storytelling

Opening Prayer

Pray for the grace to glimpse the patterns of the Spirit working in the details of your life.

Prayer Text

Then the LORD said: Go out and stand on the mountain before the LORD; the LORD will pass by. There was a strong and violent wind rending the mountains and crushing rocks before the LORD—but the LORD was not in the wind; after the wind, an earthquake—but the LORD was not in the earthquake; after the earthquake, fire—but the LORD was not in the fire; after the fire, a light silent sound. When he heard this, Elijah hid his face in his cloak and went out and stood at the entrance of the cave. A voice said to him, Why are you here, Elijah? (1 Kings 19:11–13)

Reflection Exercise

- Consider what details of your own story appear as "light, silent sounds." Do you pay attention to these, or are you consumed solely by the great storms in your life?
- How do these small details embedded in your story point to larger values? Can you articulate what these values are—and what they point to? Can you share these stories with others and help them come to share your values?

Conversation

Think back on your day. Choose a single detail. Spend time talking with God about what this detail means to you. Ask God what it might mean for your life and for the dreams God has for you.

Journal

Spend time writing out these details from your life. Start wherever feels most comfortable in your story; review just today, or begin with your earliest memory. As you write out details that might go unnoticed, try to discern patterns. Where has God been consistent in your life?

— 4 —

Caves and Cannonballs

There are events in every life that alter the trajectory of that person's story. Some events are sudden, unlooked for, and jarring: a terrible injury, the sudden inheritance of wealth, or the unexpected arrival of an important person. Some events span days, months, or even years but are no less significant: the blossoming of a relationship, the acquisition of a degree, or perhaps the slow decline of a loved one.

Regardless of the event—good or bad—these moments in our stories demand that we recalibrate. Are we going in the right direction? Have we missed or ignored something important? Do we need to reassess how we look at ourselves and others?

Often, these are the moments that we look back on years later and say, "If this hadn't happened, I wouldn't be the person I am today." These are the moments that are pivotal to our understanding of who we are and who we might yet become. Accepting these moments is necessary to accepting ourselves. Our stories can bring no healing otherwise.

So, what moments in your story have been catalysts for change, for self-discovery, for challenge and growth? Naming these moments and identifying what they can mean for our stories will be the work of this chapter.

Time to Throw in the Towel

I watched as the little boy's flip-flop got caught in the current and whisked around the bend in the river. Tears welled up in his eyes, but the middle of the river was not the place to cry. Instead, he braced those now half-bare feet against the rocks, determined that his other flip-flop not meet a similar fate.

I was, myself, in a peculiar situation: accompanying a band of Bolivian children on a field trip. It was an experience for which I was not well prepared. I'd been to my share of science museums, aquariums, parks, and monuments. But a field trip that included an outing to the middle of a rushing river was definitely new. A little adventure within an adventure, or so I had hoped.

The whole thing had been a chance to escape my day-to-day routine in Santa Cruz, and I had eagerly volunteered. The days in the city were hot, the living conditions sparse, and my energy levels sagging. Three months or so had passed since my volunteer experience began, and I still felt uncomfortable, out of place, and inadequate. So many of my friends were on their own volunteer years, or had served one or more in the past, and each told stories of the moment when things just *clicked*. They felt at home. At peace. As though they were among their own family, reluctant to leave even when their service period was up.

I was still waiting to hear that *click*. In fact, I was unsure if I was even wearing the right kind of seat belt, so I jumped at any opportunity to shake things up. I just needed that *one* thing to work, that *one* thing to fall into place. Then I'd be able to see clearly. Then it would all make sense.

I don't remember how my name came up for that ill-advised field trip. I typically spent more time with teenagers, struggling to learn their dance moves or kick a soccer ball straight in my baggy cargo pants and layers of bug spray. These young kids, kindergarteners at best, were something else entirely. I couldn't even *talk* with them. At least with the older kids, I could pretend I was passing on some wisdom, garbled in my unique brand of Spanish.

It will be like a retreat, I had told myself. *An encounter with God. A chance to get away and reflect.* Despite being sent to Santa Cruz, a city in the southwest of Bolivia, by the Salesian sisters to work with the Salesian priests, I was both the only American and the only practicing Catholic in the volunteer house. The communal spirituality nights or lofty theological conversations that I knew my peers in other service programs were having were in short supply here. Just conversing in English was a luxury; Spanish was the *lingua franca* in our community of Europeans. I should have anticipated as much.

At any rate, watching that little boy's flip-flop sail down the river marked a pivotal moment in my Bolivian adventure. I helped my Bolivian colleague hold tight to those kids as we made our way back across the river, the adventure of the moment deflated, fear of real danger foremost in our minds. We marched our wet selves back to the orphanage, our temporary residence, and endured the scolding from the local nun. Then the kids ran off to play soccer—*fútbol*—and I sat alone on the steps overlooking the small courtyard, tired and thoughtful.

Maybe I wasn't cut out for this.

All those college classes, the awards, the praise and accolades from professors and peers alike—I had taken it all to mean that a year of service, this time in Bolivia, would be one more success, one more grand experience, one more moment of insight that I might learn from and share with others. I was seeking a career in international relations, after all. Wasn't this the place to start?

And yet, sitting on those stairs in the orphanage, watching the kids play soccer only tore aside the veil of my inflated sense of self-worth. My Spanish had barely improved. I was no athlete. And most concerning of all, something inside me seemed to be preventing real connections with the people I'd come to accompany. I seemed to be tripping over my own desire to hear that *click*. Perhaps it was time to throw in the towel.

Cannonball Moments

A cannonball moment, the Ignatian tradition suggests, is a moment of paradox: extreme agony coupled with profound opportunity. We are faced with real trauma—and yet, invited to imagine a next step, the transformation of tragedy. It's a painful moment, one that knocks you off your feet, as it did for Saint Ignatius. It spins you around, challenges your preconceived assumptions, and provides a glimpse of a new way forward. If we allow it, a cannonball moment becomes a point of conversion.

The word *conversion* is rife with religious significance, positive and negative. Quite simply, it's a turning *away from* one way of being and turning *toward* a new one. If healing is our goal, then our story is a slow unfolding of this work. We desire to turn away from practices and perspectives that harm us and others and turn toward those ways of being that make us better able to flourish. Bound up in that turning is a serious examination of self: past, present, and future. Building on our previous chapters, we ask what we stand for, why we stand for it, and what kind of person we hope to be as a result. We examine our values in light of our world, our beliefs, and the needs of our community.

Conversion isn't a once-and-done deal, though we're tempted to think of it as such. Conversion demands *continued renewal* of our commitment and a continued living out of our values. We're called to constantly exercise those muscles or run the risk of letting the values stagnate, decay, and become forgotten. We are tempted to think of the cannonball moment—that moment of conversion—as akin to a wedding. How beautiful, striking, memorable! And yet, I can tell you that the real work—and real joy—of marriage is in the daily living out of those vows, their continual renewal. It's the same with conversion.

There's another term akin to a cannonball moment that might be helpful to our reflection: a *disorienting dilemma*. This notion comes from transformative education theory. The protagonist is disoriented—casting about, confused, unable to leverage the usual tools and insights—by a dilemma, some problem, issue, new experience, or unforeseen scenario. With those usual tools rendered useless, whatever they may be, our disoriented protagonist finds him- or herself forced into the uncomfortable realm of having to try something new and of having to admit that perhaps he or she didn't have all the answers right that first go-round. This confrontation with ourselves and our inability to respond to the moment is disorienting. And it's the perfect opportunity for change.

A disorienting dilemma, much like a call to conversion, brings about a shift. Humbled, we admit to our own humanness and commit to building something new. And if we respond in a healthy way, we become eager to demonstrate our newfound knowledge and our newly embraced perspective by taking action. More on that later.

Does this mean that those values we held so dearly in the past were wrong? Perhaps. Or perhaps they just needed to expand and grow, as we all do. But without understanding what they are and why they matter to the person we are becoming, we can't take corrective action. And a disorienting dilemma—a conversion opportunity—might pass us by.

• • •

For me, still struggling with my life in Bolivia, all this high-and-mighty thinking was unhelpful. The cannonball was striking me again and again, but I still hadn't realized it. I was stuck on whether or not I'd made the right decision to go there in the first place.

Saint Ignatius cautions us against making any drastic decisions from a place of *desolation*. And how clear it was that I was stuck in such a place! "Desolation drains us of energy," Jesuit priest Dean Brackley, SJ, wrote in his spiritual classic *The Call to Discernment in Troubled Times*. "We are attracted to the gospel of self-satisfaction. We feel drawn backward into ourselves. . . . Desolation generates negative thinking. It narrows our vision."[5]

It's important to recognize desolation for what it is. While it is unwise to make any sudden life-altering decisions from such a place, it is also quite dangerous to allow the status quo to persist. There is a need to lean in to that desolation so as to break through to consolation, which "releases new energies, widens our vision and directs us beyond ourselves. . . . In consolation, the subterranean river within us overflows into conscious life, endowing ordinary feelings with a heightened tone and fullness."[6] We must remember that the Holy Spirit is still at work. The Holy Spirit never narrows our vision. Does this activity of the Spirit echo in your own life?

Saint Ignatius—the Basque soldier known as Iñigo de Loyola—didn't start out as a saint. But key to his story—key to *any* story—is his cannonball moment. The man literally got hit by a cannonball on the field of battle, while defending Pamplona from the French. His pride wouldn't allow him to surrender, and countless lives were lost as a result. Both of his legs were injured badly, and the citadel fell to the enemy. The wounded Iñigo was brought back to Loyola where his legs were operated on.

> "With him being in a very bad state and calling doctors and surgeons from many quarters, they judged that the leg had to be pulled apart again and the bones set in their places again, saying that, because they had been badly set on the other occasion or because they had become dislocated on the journey they were out of place and in this state it couldn't heal."[7]

It's an ugly process. His legs don't heal well, he discovers that one is permanently shorter than the other, and he opts to undergo *another* surgery. He couldn't imagine returning to his courtly life with such an unsightly limp. The surgery is unsuccessful, and his ego never recovers. How often our own ego prevents us from recognizing the opportunity at hand.

But laid out on a bed, wounded and struggling to find renewed purpose, Ignatius discovers that God has come to him. As the former soldier and future saint reflects on his life, on those things that he *thought* brought him joy—fighting battles, knightly courtship—he finds himself feeling empty, looking inward, desolate. When he turns to the only books at hand—a book on the saints and another on the life of Christ—he finds himself energized, consoled. In that darkest of moments, God shows Ignatius a new way forward. That cannonball ended one chapter and began another. Traumatic though it was, the Spirit spoke through Ignatius's own memories, experiences, *stories*, and pointed to something new. The Spirit is doing nothing less in our lives.

That is only the beginning of Ignatius's story. Like him, we have our own cannonball moments. But our stories aren't written in the brokenness caused by the cannonball. They are only partly inspired by our near-death pledges to change. It's in the slow, steady, painful struggle of piecing together our new life in a new direction that the story emerges. It happens when we reflect on where we've been and discern where we're being invited to go. This is the healing work of storytelling.

Resolved to give his life to God, Ignatius sets out to lay his sword at the foot of Our Lady of Montserrat, the Black Madonna statue housed in a church in the mountains not far from Barcelona, Spain. This very tangible act is a physical manifestation of the spiritual conversion that took place on that hospital bed. From here, we typically hear of Ignatius's spiritual experiences in a cave in Manresa, a nearby town. It is from these experiences that he drafts the *Spiritual Exercises*, the foundational text of Ignatian spirituality.

Except his autobiography mentions no cave. Instead, in painstaking details, we walk with Ignatius the pilgrim through eleven months in Manresa, a much longer sojourn than anticipated on his way to Jerusalem. We experience his doubts, his inner turmoil. We wonder, with him, if this saintly life is all it's cut out to be.

His spiritual insights are hard won: He spends time offering spiritual direction to some of the local townsfolk, but a good many pages of his reflections on Manresa are dedicated to his ongoing wrestling with doubt and even suicide. It turned out that the life of a saint was even harder than that of a soldier:

> The difficulty of his way of life would present itself to him, as if it was being said to him inside his soul: "And how are *you* going to be able to stand this life the seventy years you're meant to live?" . . . While he was in these thoughts there often used to come over him, with great impetus, temptations to throw himself out of a large opening which the room he was in had.[8]

Whether he was in a literal cave or not, it's not difficult to see in Ignatius a man who feels trapped in darkness, walls pressing in, grasping for some glimpse of light.

Fortunately, desolation gives way to consolation.

• • •

When I returned home to my parents' house from Bolivia, some six or so months after the incident with the flip-flop and the river, things still were not falling into place. I had stuck it out in Bolivia, though, recognizing that the status quo couldn't continue, I did change service sites. I found some consolation in the new site: fellow volunteers who shared my values and priorities, a group of Salesian sisters who inspired me, and work I felt I could meaningfully contribute to. But that aha moment never came. I started applying for jobs a month before returning home.

One after another the rejection letters came. The international relations organizations I applied to in Washington, DC, and New York City turned me down. My qualifications, while good, weren't good enough to set me apart for jobs at the State Department. I was hesitant to look too deeply into any opportunities that would take me abroad again. And I had no money for graduate school, if I could even have settled on what to study.

The months rolled on, and no job offers came. And I began to feel hopeless, that I had made a wrong turn somewhere. I mulled over my undergraduate days, thinking on the retreat talks I gave, the papers I submitted, the cohort I had established, and the praise I'd gotten as a result. Were my best days behind me? Surely I was destined for something more.

Going to Bolivia was just a single line on my résumé. What really mattered wasn't that I had lived in South America for a handful of months. It was *why* I had lived in South America, and what it meant for what I was going to do now. How many of us focus too much on *what* we've done—and how impressive we think it to be—rather than on *why* we've done it?

The answers were tough. I wanted to serve in Bolivia because I wanted to manifest the kind of self-giving love I believe we're all called to. Unfortunately, I focused on my own needs and desires the entire time.

I wanted to live in a different place, learn a different culture and language, and make friends with people I'd never otherwise meet. But I went assuming that I had something amazing to offer. Rather than listen, I spoke. I was the savior of these Bolivians! And when everyone didn't immediately realize that, I turned inward, awkward, and removed.

I wanted to challenge myself, live in solidarity with the vulnerable, and experience the kind of discomfort that so many of us religiously avoid. As soon as it got hard, though, as soon as it didn't go my way, I panicked. As a result, I never acclimated.

• • •

The lesson wasn't that I was a failure, though it was tempting to assume as much. The lesson wasn't even that Bolivia had been a mistake. Rather, here I was, presented with the truth that the values I professed to believe were in fact out of line with the way I lived. That when confronted with a very tangible way to demonstrate those values, I faltered. Why?

I was so busy judging my Bolivian experience—so busy, by extension, judging the Bolivian people, my fellow volunteers, my program—that I'd forgotten to look long and hard at myself.

"Why do you notice the splinter in your brother's eye, but do not perceive the wooden beam in your own?" Jesus asks. "Remove the wooden beam from your eye first; then you will see clearly" (Luke 6:41–42).

The cannon was aimed squarely at my ego, my inflated sense of self. And the cannonball moment, though a slow process that spanned my time in Bolivia and the many months after my return, demanded that I rely less on my sense of self-worth, my strengths and insights, and look more to both the giftedness and the neediness of those around me.

For all of us, healing comes in recognizing that we are not simply the sum of our actions, of what we *do*. Cannonball moments often reflect how little control we really have—even in our own stories! When the ego is put in its proper place, we have the opportunity to reflect not on *what* we do for others but on *why* we do it. *Why* we do things, guided by our values, is an invitation to contemplate who we *are* for others. Stripped of our accomplishments, we have nothing but our very selves, broken down and healing from the cannonball strike.

As is true for any cannonball moment, this is a lesson I need to return to repeatedly, a value muscle I have to continue to flex, or I risk returning to my Bolivian-savior self.

• • •

Ignatius's time in that supposed cave helped him crystalize those things that were essential to his spiritual life and that would guide and govern his story. The contrast between what *was* and what *might be* was crucial. The grappling that Ignatius did with his own past and present could be done only by honestly looking at his failures.

But how do we know that we fail if we don't know what success looks like? We hold up the mirror of our faith tradition, our beliefs, to get a sense of what is right and wrong, better and best. We develop values from our families, our friends, our communities, and we use those values to make sense of the kind of person we should be. We weigh those values, putting them on like a new coat. Do they fit? How do they make us feel? Have we outgrown them?

Those values help us respond to a cannonball moment. Saint Ignatius's values were steeped in courtly duty and chivalry. They weren't necessarily bad values for the time. But they weren't the values that ultimately got him to his best self; they weren't the values that helped him level up.

Though I didn't actually end my service in Bolivia early, it was a shorter period of service than that of most of my peers. The decision, for me, turned on my younger brother's high school graduation party. It seems almost silly now, but this was a big family event, and missing it seemed impossible. I was needed to help prepare, no? Certainly, it was important to my brother, to my parents. And nine months was plenty of time to get the *experience* I was looking for in Bolivia. So went my decision-making process.

All these years later, who can say if another three months or fifteen months would have made any difference for me or for the Bolivian community I was supposed to serve. Perhaps I made a mistake. And it haunted me those months following my return to the United States. I assumed it was the reason why nothing was *clicking*: Bolivia, jobs, anything.

And yet, buried here is something essential: the story of a value that anchors my life. What is it? Family. Whether or not a high school graduation is worth returning early for from Latin America, for me, family is. And family is what this anecdote points to. Recognizing that value in the past sheds light on its importance in the present: how it governs the job I have today, the priorities I set in my schedule, the limitations I accept, and the goals I strive for. And that very arduous act of actually *moving*—of getting on a plane and flying home—reflects what I do today for my family: getting in a car and driving to be present at birthday parties and deathbeds alike.

None of this is to say that staying in Bolivia for a full year, for two years, would have been the wrong decision. And it certainly isn't to say that those who do miss family weddings or funerals have made the wrong choice. Jesus himself has some strong words for those who put family above the Gospel.

But as I look back at what I brought with me to Bolivia, a value formed by my family and buried within me but which I eventually embraced, I find some consolation. Because today it manifests itself when I shut off my computer and go play with my daughters rather than send just one more email. It comes to the fore when I opt to call my grandparents rather than scroll through YouTube. And it's what motivates me to prioritize the protection of other families: migrants, refugees, the vulnerable, and the impoverished.

That value translates into two little girls who feel the love of their father. A couple of old folks who felt the love of their grandson before sudden, crippling illnesses. And countless people who are impacted by how I spend my money, my time, and my votes.

As you consider your own cannonball moment, what are the values against which you judge it? Where did those values come from? And are they the right values—the right standards—against which to assess your learning from the cannonball strike?

• • •

Though scholars question whether or not Saint Ignatius wrote the Spiritual Exercises in a cave, I like the image. It reminds me of one of my favorite scenes from one of my favorite movies: *Star Wars*.

In *The Empire Strikes Back*, Luke Skywalker travels to Dagobah to learn the ways of the Jedi from Jedi Master Yoda. Yoda is not what Luke expected. Luke assumes he's looking for someone powerful, physically impressive, and obviously wise. And yet, he meets Yoda, a shriveled old green thing that speaks in riddles and can barely walk on his own.

We know Yoda to be the very Jedi Master that Luke seeks. Luke steps into a disorienting dilemma. His assumptions fail him, and he's left disappointed, confused, irritated.

And then Yoda sends him into the cave.

Luke has been training—and failing—at his Jedi work for a while now, and his successes are mixed. He's tired. Yoda's ways are not Luke's preferred methods. He's not even being clear about what separates the dark side from the light. And this cave just seems like one more weird thing.

"What's in there?" Luke asks.

"Only what you take with you," is Yoda's response.[9]

Deep in that cave, Luke encounters a vision of Darth Vader—his enemy, and his father. He battles the vision, strikes Vader down, and discovers—as Vader's mask explodes—that Luke's own face is behind it.

What Luke took into that cave was his sense of right and wrong—his values. They helped him respond to the needs of the moment. But they also helped him see the potential dangers in the paths ahead of him and pinpoint the faults he carried with him even into the present.

That's all any of us has ready to hand when we face a cannonball moment and find ourselves disoriented, with dark, cavernous walls pressing in all around. The question *Who am I?* is answered in moments such as these, when we reflect on where we have succeeded and where we have failed.

The fruit of these moments—the values that crystalize, that are purified in the fires of cannonball moments—are what we then have to offer others as we seek to share our stories.

An Exercise in Ignatian Storytelling

Opening Prayer

Pray for the grace to welcome the disorientation that comes with new opportunities—and the wisdom to respond in humility as you seek a new way forward.

Prayer Text

Then [Jesus] said, "A man had two sons, and the younger son said to his father, 'Father, give me the share of your estate that should come to me.' So the father divided the property between them. After a few days, the younger son collected all his belongings and set off to a distant country where he squandered his inheritance on a life of dissipation. When he had freely spent everything, a severe famine struck that country, and he found himself in dire need. So he hired himself out to one of the local citizens who sent him to his farm to tend the swine. And he longed to eat his fill of the pods on which the swine fed, but nobody gave him any. Coming to his senses he thought, 'How many of my father's hired workers have more than enough food to eat, but here am I, dying from hunger. I shall get up and go to my father and I shall say to him, 'Father, I have sinned against heaven and against you. I no longer deserve to be called your son; treat me as you would treat one of your hired workers." So he got up and went back to his father. While he was still a long way off, his father caught sight of him, and was filled with compassion. He ran to his son, embraced him and kissed him. His son said to him, 'Father, I have sinned against heaven and against you; I no longer deserve to be called your son.' But his father ordered his servants, 'Quickly bring the finest robe and put it on him; put a ring on his finger and sandals on his feet. Take the fattened calf and slaughter it. Then let us celebrate with a feast, because this son of mine was dead, and has come to life again; he was lost, and has been found.'" (Luke 15:11–24)

Reflection Exercise

- When have you faced a disorienting dilemma? Did you respond by embracing a new path, or did you dig into the old paths you'd walked before?

- Which characters in your story have helped you work through cannonball moments? How have you responded to them? How might you respond to such individuals in the future?

Conversation

Place yourself in the story above; you are the prodigal son. Ask God to help you recognize moments when you have been tempted to continue eating the slop given to the pigs. What compelled you in those moments? Ask God to help you recall moments when you stood up and identified the need for change. What moved within you?

Journal

Select a cannonball moment from your prayer experience. Describe how you felt immediately after recognizing the need for change, for conversion. What values drove you? What values did you encounter in those around you?

Part 1 Reprise
Answering "Who Am I?"

I confess that racial justice was never high on my list of priorities—the privilege of a white man in the United States. But in 2015, after the murder of Freddie Gray in the back of a police van, racial injustice was very much front and center on the streets of Baltimore. It was my first semester of graduate school, and I was in the last night of classes at American University in Washington, DC. I'd been commuting back and forth between campus and our downtown Baltimore apartment a few times a week, and my attention had been on my final projects.

To my rather inattentive eyes, the riots that erupted seemed sudden, surprising. And I remember scrolling through Twitter that night in class growing fearful. These were dark scenes playing out on familiar streets—only blocks away from my wife, who was home alone.

I left class early only to stop at a friend's house in DC to watch the news, waiting out what I assumed was a blockade of Baltimore. Why was it taking so long to secure the city? Finally, hours later, I zipped up I-95 and arrived in a city that was eerily quiet.

I was angry, scared, upset. But my wife simply opened the door and offered me a brownie. "Did you have something to protect yourself with?" I asked, flustered. "No," she replied. "I didn't think it would come to anything like that. But if it did, I'd just offer brownies."

I remember being quite shocked—angry, even—by our difference in approach. Alli was being silly. Couldn't she see that? But as the days unfolded and the panic in the city turned to peaceful protests, something changed in me.

I realized that I was wrong.

And I did something I'd never done before: I joined the protests. I took to the streets. I added my voice to the countless others proclaiming that Black Lives Matter. And I began to research, to learn about the history of racism and injustice that continues to play out to this day. I began to recognize the blind spots in my own perspective—and the harm I had done, that I was continuing to do, even if unintentionally.

In this first section of our extended reflection on Ignatian storytelling, we've examined the role that values play in shaping and sharing our stories. I've shared three Ignatian practices that can help us in discovering these values and that can serve as a foundation for stories that reconcile.

As I reflect on my own stories—and on the above story in particular—these three Ignatian storytelling practices converge in a quite illustrative way. It was this convergence that transformed me from a graduate student shaking his fist angrily at what he perceived to be looters and rioters on the television to a peaceful protestor on the streets of Baltimore. Let's take them in reverse.

First, the cannonball moment. Freddie Gray's death was devastating to the city. We were once again reminded of the scourge of racial injustice in our institutions and of the importance of mobilizing for a more just response. The effect it had on the city couldn't be missed, but it certainly was possible to retreat inward or simply hold the ideological line. Like so many privileged others, I had to *choose* to engage with this moment. It wouldn't have been all that hard to shut the blinds, turn off the news, and ignore the protests.

Fortunately for me, I was able to look to my wife's example. A cannonball moment for some is just par for the course for others. It was helpful, then, for me to have someone whom I trust to help me work through the moment—with all its anger, uncertainty, learning, and self-discovery—and who could serve as a sounding board who wasn't afraid to check my privilege.

Second, a long-view examen. Even before Gray's death and the subsequent protests, I was fascinated by people power: the mass mobilization of movements to affect social change and overthrow systems of oppression.

Reflecting on my undergraduate work, again and again I found that my past self had written and thought about the role the grassroots play in toppling oppressive regimes around the world. The history of the Sandinista Revolution in Nicaragua—and the role the Catholic Church played—had always struck me as powerful. I'd even traveled to Nicaragua as part of an undergraduate course to learn more. I had spent a lot of time praying with and researching theologies of liberation, and I found myself particularly unsettled by the idea that we are all called to be liberated—oppressed and oppressors alike—from the systems that oppress *all* of us; no one is spared. And, in preparing for my time in Bolivia, I had been inspired and somewhat frightened by the recent history of social change through protests on issues ranging from the nationalization of water to economic insecurity.

As I looked back, I realized that all this stuff was in the background of the past five years of my life. And here I stood with it at my front door. How could I not embrace the moment? How could I not try to learn more? If I had truly gone to Bolivia to learn from the needs of the people, how could I ignore those needs when they manifested themselves in my own community?

Third, Scripture's challenge. I found myself at that protest—and at subsequent ones—because I knew that's what Jesus would do. Jesus who stands with the marginalized, who prioritizes the needs of the vulnerable, who blesses the meek and peacemakers.

Jesuit priest Greg Boyle, SJ, the founder of Homeboy Industries, said it best in his reflection on the Beatitudes: "The Beatitudes is not a spirituality, after all. It's a geography. It tells us where to stand." Just like Jesus, we have to put our bodies in play, put ourselves at risk, stand where the need is greatest. And that was literally what the protest represented to me. Standing with those who were most vulnerable, hearing the cries of the poor and the downtrodden and the oppressed.

That's basic Scripture.

Based on this reflection, I might answer the question *Who am I?* in the following way: I'm someone who cares about justice and peace, who attempts to prioritize the needs of the most vulnerable in a way that dismantles unjust systems. I'm also someone who recognizes his own privilege and is not afraid to admit when he was wrong and to learn from those around him.

These are all value statements, things that matter to me. They give a glimpse of who I am, and they underline the story I shared above.

But we're not called to live alone in this world; we're not simply meant to gaze inward and discover something about ourselves for the good of ourselves alone. We need to go out, to expand our horizon, to look up and out and see the other people with whom we share space.

We must now answer the question, *Whose am I?* In so doing, we will begin to see how these seemingly random stories can begin to stitch together a larger narrative that might restore relationships among people and creation—and bring about God's dream for humanity.

— PART 2 —

WHOSE AM I?

The auditorium was packed with high school students. A little rowdy, too. The praise and worship band had just wrapped up their last song, and the first retreat talk was set to begin. The lights dimmed ever so slightly, and the band's guitarist set down his instrument and stepped up to the mic. A hush settled over the room.

I didn't know what to expect. I was fifteen years old and on my first retreat. My parish youth group had organized a small delegation, and the six of us sat huddled together, excited. I was a little hesitant, too. Faith was important to me as a high schooler. My mom managed our parish office, and, as a result, I volunteered at church events, knew the priests pretty well, and even earned some extra money answering phones in the office on weeknights. I felt like I had a behind-the-scenes look at Catholicism, at church, at what it meant to be a good person. I wasn't sure what more I had to learn.

But these retreats were supposed to be life changing. I'd known friends who came back from them with entirely different perspectives on life, on God, on everything. Could such a transformation happen to me?

The guitarist began his talk, and though he was a bit older than me, he seemed to have had a life more or less like mine. Catholic school, loving family, good friends. But then, things took a turn. He talked about his addiction to alcohol, to sex, his dabbling in drugs.

He regaled us with how dark his life had become, the downward spiral of a supposedly sinful man. He painted a picture of absolute rock bottom. And then, Jesus saved him. God pulled him back from the brink, and now, here he stood before us, a better man.

People applauded. People cried. People went absolutely nuts. I didn't know what to think.

My faith told me that God could do anything, that a bit of spiritual discipline could alter the trajectory of a person's life, so I didn't doubt that this twentysomething guitar player could find his way back to sobriety with the help of his faith. But this talk wasn't a fact-finding expedition; it was meant to connect with me as a young high school student. And none of what he said made any sense to my lived experience. I didn't have a sex addiction; I didn't even have a girlfriend. Drinking and drugs were foreign to me. His depiction of rock bottom was frightening and hard to imagine. Was this the necessary path of life? Was this what it meant to be a good person—to lose control of yourself only to then find yourself again in God?

I remember walking outside that night, staring into the cold Pennsylvania evening. Was I a *bad* person because I hadn't had these seemingly problematic experiences? Was my *own* experience invalidated somehow because I hadn't? Or was that simply my destiny, a goal I had not yet reached? My young mind was more confused post-transformative-retreat talk than before.

All these years later, and my life's journey has not taken me along the route that the guitarist described that night. That doesn't make me any better or any worse; it just makes me, me. It points to the differences in our stories. It renders no value judgment.

And yet, I've seen this same thing happen again and again. I've gone on my fair share of retreats in the years since. I've led retreats and written more than a few retreat talks. I've formed and mentored groups of retreat leaders and helped them craft their own talks, exploring their stories. So I know how tempting it is to mine your life for the most extreme, dark, heart-wrenching moment there is—and to then point to how you made it through.

This might make for a compelling story, but it doesn't necessarily fit into our Ignatian storytelling framework. (Think back to that story of hope from Vietnam we discussed in the first chapter.) In fact, I think it's dangerous if not handled properly.

Too often, these stories that live on life's extremes miss their mark. A retreat talk is meant to help a retreatant discover God at work in their own life and continue, or begin, the work of healing broken relationships: with self, with God, with neighbor, with family. Insofar as you can tell a story from your life that helps a person undertake that task, you've accomplished the job. There is much to be learned from stories of addiction, abuse, and trauma. Those stories have important roles to play in helping others overcome their own darkness, and it's often healing, vital work for those who have had such experiences to accompany others in making sense of their own.

The danger in these kinds of stories, though, that point to *me* rather than to *us* is their unintended effect of telling listeners that they themselves have no story worth telling. For a long time after that retreat, I assumed my life was boring, that I had no story. I struggled with normal teenager stuff but nothing to the extent of what that guitarist had gone through. What would I even talk about if asked?

This, too, presents an issue in sharing our stories. Stories do need to hold the interest of our listeners. All good stories contain tension and conflict. When and how does the protagonist respond to a problem? What decisions ensue? That problem may be a drug addiction. But it might be something more commonplace: a breakdown in communication within a relationship; an unforeseen financial burden; the challenges inherent in caring for an aging parent. Or, for a high school student on retreat, responding to rejection in a blossoming romance.

The answer again lies in shared values and shared experiences. We bring others into our stories, and we keep them there because they feel safe, they feel seen, and they know that their story is understood and appreciated. Choose details that bridge your experience to that of others.

The story you have to share may contain some dramatic or scandalous detail that naturally pricks up the ears of your listener. But just because your story doesn't contain such a chapter doesn't mean you don't have a story.

How sad to be told that you have no story! I've worked with countless retreat leaders, some of them good friends, who nearly backed out of giving a retreat talk because they didn't think they had anything worth saying. I hope that if nothing else, the first section of this book has put that lie to rest: God is at work in every life, often in the mundane moments, and we all have something worth saying.

In this section, I propose three Ignatian spiritual practices to help us, as storytellers, direct our storytelling to the common needs of our communities:

1. **First, we confront the reality of disagreement.** Our stories at times collide with the stories of others. What do we do in such a situation? Is there a way forward? We employ prophetic listening. Rather than assume a combative stance aimed at defeating our counterpart's story with our own, we *listen*. We listen for common ground, a place from which we might set off together. In that place where our stories overlap, we may find shared hurts and the opportunity to point through the disagreement to a shared healing.

2. **Next, we address our own ego in storytelling**. It is tempting to serve our own ends in the stories we tell, often at the expense of others. In this chapter, we explore the Ignatian principle *agere*

contra—to act against—as a way to recognize and resist this temptation.

3. **Finally, we meditate on the Two Standards**—that of Christ and that of the enemy—an exercise crafted by Saint Ignatius in his *Spiritual Exercises*. We do so for the purpose of discerning how our stories are told against the backdrop of systems and structures inherent in our society—and often forgotten, despite the harm they can cause.

In the end, the needs of every community are different, and we as Ignatian storytellers must be discerning and flexible enough to recognize those needs, building upon the insights we've gleaned from tending to our *own* woundedness. Indeed, if we're telling our stories well, we should be calling forth the unique *strengths* embedded in ourselves and our communities, helping members recognize those sources of self-empowerment. We look to our values—what energizes us—and seek synergy with those who are listening.

As we explore these practices, reflect on the needs of the common good. As we craft and share our stories, never forget that we belong to others, to a community, and not solely to ourselves.

— 5 —

Prophetic Listening

It's frustrating when people don't listen. If I had a nickel for the number of times I've said to my three-year-old daughter, "You're not *listening*; you have to do a better job of *listening*," she'd be through college and well on her way to buying her first house. Of course, we implore a child to listen because there's something important she needs to know: Don't push your sister. Do pick up your toys. Don't drink the bathwater. Do finish your peas.

After reflecting on the question *Who am I?* in the first section of this book and discovering the many stories that make up your unique answer, it's quite possible that you, too, feel as though you could share so many important things with others if only they'd *listen*. Those values you've found to be at the foundation of your life have done so much good for you. Certainly, you should make sure others know the good they might do for them, too, right?

This chapter is about listening. But it's not about making other people listen to us. It's about ensuring that *we're* listening to *them*. It's about recognizing that even when values seem to be at an irreconcilable impasse, we're still called to listen first. Think of the care with which we journeyed through your story in the preceding chapters. Don't others deserve that same care? Doesn't God look upon the utter uniqueness of everyone—different from one another as we may be—with the same gaze of love?

We will practice that patient listening, but we'll do so in a way that accompanies others on their journeys of self-discovery and self-acceptance. We'll enter the stories of others, recognizing our shared humanity. And we'll practice what I'm calling *prophetic* listening: a listening ear that courageously points to those things in another's story that are important and perhaps overlooked. This process of Ignatian storytelling isn't meant to leave people as they are but to help them recognize and become the best version of themselves, the person God dreams they'll be.

Same Words, Different Questions

I spent a good amount of time in Boston, Massachusetts, the two years following my return from Bolivia. Alli lived there, having returned from her own period of service in Ecuador, and we would trade off who had to make the drive down I-95. Our commitment to those long drives or short plane rides reflected our commitment to one another, and marriage was a frequent and comfortable topic of conversation.

But the fact that we knew our college romance was headed toward a more permanent state didn't mean we didn't still stumble upon areas of uncertainty and contention where our relationship was concerned.

"What are you thinking about becoming Catholic?" I asked sheepishly. We were riding home on the "T," Boston's subway system. It was a still-unresolved conversation that had begun years ago when we were undergraduate students.

For me as an undergraduate, the question was a deal breaker. My understanding of my own faith was a key value upon which my worldview rested, and there was little room for compromise. When I started dating Alli, someone who has always lived a vibrant Christian—though decidedly not *Catholic* Christian—faith, I bought and read book after book to help me learn what I needed to know to convert her to Catholicism. We talked late into many nights, unable to find common theological ground on the issues that typically divide Protestants and Catholics: the role of the saints, the pope and Mary, the sacraments, and the role of women.

But our seat on that T car was separated from those late nights by years of lived experience, a deepening faith in a God of inclusion rather than division and an ever-growing love for and understanding of each other. The question I asked then, though perhaps made up of the same words, expressed a very different sentiment. It was an articulation of something that I knew was important to me and an invitation to hear more about what was important to her. It was a willingness to begin to carve out something new, the collaborative fruits of two people rather than the domineering demands of one.

Nevertheless, she surprised me. "I've signed up for RCIA," she said, referring to the Rite of Christian Initiation of Adults, the process through which someone becomes Catholic.

I was surprised, perhaps even a bit relieved. "Really? Why?"

Alli paused, a thoughtful look coming over her face. Her response didn't reflect any sort of change in theological disposition, nor did she say, "Well, Eric, you had it right the whole time." No—in fact, her response has been one that I've continued to chew on all these years later. She articulated something I could not, something I had not thought *to* articulate until that moment, a value that I had been holding but unable to see.

"I want our marriage to be a sacrament," she said. "I want the wedding to be more than a ceremony. I want God present in that unique, tangible way—in the sacrament of the Eucharist—as we begin this new chapter together."

The Story of Us

When I talked about storytelling in my course on nonprofit public relations, the conversation often veered into convincing a given organization's target audience of the good that the nonprofit is trying to accomplish. The thinking goes like this: We're doing something good; why *wouldn't* you want to be part of it? These stories become something of a bludgeon with which to hit an unsuspecting potential donor. And it's often unsuccessful.

The trick is crafting a shared identity—a story of "us"—that affirms the fact that we're in this *together*.[10] We're equals at the table. It's not so much convincing you to do what I want you to do as much as it's reminding both of us that we share a value, a way of seeing the world, that might help us come together and do something as one. To tell a story of us, you have to *create* "us." "Us" is built upon shared identity, shared purpose, shared values, not unlike a marriage. It's not always easy or simple, pleasant or obvious. Again, not unlike a marriage.

This same line of thinking applies to us in our storytelling. You may have succeeded at doing the good work of self-reflection, of identifying what gets you out of bed in the morning, *why* you feel called to live the way you do. You're rightly excited to share that story with others.

But then, what happens when you meet resistance? What happens when your significant other doesn't respond enthusiastically to your perspective on things of importance to you—for example, your faith, your family, your worldview? Do you blame the other person? Do you give up? Do you assume that something is wrong with your story or with that of your companion?

The answer is not simple. There's a difference between sharing our own truths and using our truths to manipulate others—perhaps manipulating the truth itself. Stories are powerful and can be dangerous. It's not hard to look out at the world and see the impact that manipulative, self-seeking narratives have on the direction that communities and countries take. Sometimes there are clear differences in the stories' trajectories, and sometimes common ground appears all but impossible to find. Sometimes we have to call a bad story what it is. Sometimes we have to act against what is dangerous and morally repugnant.

But we hope not to begin there. That's why it's important to listen. Saint Ignatius offers a helpful way of starting these conversations, of building *us*. We must actively look for that common humanity. We want to discover and heal what is broken; so often, what is broken in us is broken in others. Together we might make one another whole. Remember, we're asking our stories to grapple with the question *Whose am I?* We need to wade into the mess of relationships through our storytelling.

Saint Ignatius includes a short presupposition right at the beginning of the first week of the *Spiritual Exercises*. He writes, "So that the director and the exercitant may collaborate better and with greater profit, it must be presupposed that any good Christian has to be more ready to justify than to condemn a neighbor's statement."[11] Ignatius is first and foremost concerned about the relationship between the retreatant—the one who is experiencing the *Exercises*—and the director who is accompanying the retreatant. In short, Ignatius encourages each to give the other the benefit of the doubt. And when that fails, to correct the other "lovingly."

Let's pause and consider this presupposition and the potential mental roadblocks it may create in our minds, particularly as it concerns privilege. Who is being prioritized in this text? Who was being prioritized at the time of writing? Ignatius's own words seem to rule out the possibility of engaging with those of other faiths, though times have changed. He assumes that one of those shared values is that of Christianity: a Christian dealing with a Christian about Christian things. Certainly this tidy and enclosed environment can be seen in privileged communities today. I, a benefactor of certain cultural and traditional norms, may make similar assumptions about the people I'm dealing with, giving this benefit of the doubt to only those with whom I share obvious values—and perhaps with whom I share a skin color, a faith tradition, and socioeconomic status. Most significantly, I may not even realize I'm doing this.

As you reflected on your own story, did you register moments of privilege, when you were more inclined to turn a listening ear to one person over another? Perhaps you sought that listening ear from a particular person, ignoring the others already present in your company. Perhaps you even expected your story to carry more value or weight because of some personal detail that you have been led to believe is inherently more important than details found in the stories of others.

If Ignatian storytelling is to be a healing practice, it must help us shine a light on our own privileges, biases, and prejudices so as to make amends for the hurts we perhaps unknowingly caused, and then move forward, committed to not repeating the sins of the past. The hard, necessary work of discerning how to tell stories that heal—and which to share, when—is our goal here. Just because there are darker chapters in your story doesn't mean those chapters should be omitted. Rather, it's all the more important to delve into their details and understand how they've affected you. The ever-present specters of privilege and bias, of injustice and oppression must be taken seriously.

To that end, Ignatius himself helps us further elaborate on this idea of giving someone the benefit of the doubt—presupposing the good, as it were.

Prophetic Listening in History

Pope Paul III—the very pope who approved the founding of the Society of Jesus in 1540—asked Ignatius to send three Jesuits to serve as theologians at the Council of Trent. This was not yet six years after the Society had been founded, and the council itself was called to respond to the Protestant Reformation. Certainly, this was a moment in search of common ground and rife with seemingly incompatible stories.

Ignatius obliged. He sent his Jesuits with several points to consider, particularly as they found themselves associating with others with whom they may share few experiences and perspectives. Ignatius warned "if we are not on our guard and helped by God's grace, such association can be the occasion of great loss to ourselves and sometimes to everyone concerned."[12] Ignatius affirmed the importance of the kind of self-reflection and discovery we discussed in previous chapters; he wanted his Jesuits firm in their answer to the question *Who am I?* And yet he doubled down in reminding his Jesuits that this kind of work—this living and working in the world, building up of relationships, associating with those who might have very different priorities—was part and parcel of the kind of religious life to which the Jesuits had pledged themselves.

Above all, when dealing with others, Ignatius implored his Jesuits to listen humbly so as to fully understand the desires of others, to hold their own opinions lightly and not grow too attached to their own insights, and to have the faith and courage to speak up on matters of great importance.

I excerpt three of his statements below.

- Be slow to speak, and only after having first listened quietly, so that you may understand the meaning, leanings, and wishes of those who do speak. Thus you will better know when to speak and when to be silent.

- When these or other matters are under discussion, I should consider the reasons on both sides without showing any attachment to my own opinion, and try to avoid bringing dissatisfaction to anyone. . . .
- If the matters being discussed are of such a nature that you cannot or ought not be silent, then give your opinion with the greatest possible humility and sincerity, and always end with the words *salvo meliori iudicio*—with due respect for a better opinion.[13]

I used to have this letter of Ignatius's printed and at my desk. I tried to glance at his advice before every meeting I attended. *Be slow to speak, Eric. Listen. Don't grow too fond of your own opinions.*

What we're really looking at here is the necessary outpouring of his presupposition into real life. Ignatius didn't want his Jesuits to fail at the Council of Trent; he likely wanted real progress to be made in plotting next steps for the future of Christianity. And yet, he also didn't want them to lose sight of what was important to them and to God. There was a need to balance a gentle, listening ear with a prophetic voice, the courage to speak truth but also to listen humbly to opposing perspectives. And ultimately, to work together for God's greater glory and the good of all people.

As we reflect on Ignatius's words, it's tempting to assume that their application to storytelling simply means not to rock the boat. Don't offend anyone. Make nice. Appeal to the lowest common denominator.

But that would be a mistake.

When I reflect on his words, I can't help but see his great reverence for the other person, his conversational sparring partner. Nowhere in his words do we see a desire to embarrass the other, to engage in scorched-earth rhetorical warfare. Ignatius is always aware that God is at the center and that other opinions can help to inform our own.

For Ignatius, listening is key. And if we call it prophetic listening, a number of questions follow: Are we truly present to the words of the other person? Do we really hear what they're saying—the fears, concerns, and worries that may be hiding just below the surface? Do we allow ourselves to get distracted by our own biases and priorities, or do we accompany that other person in a conversation of depth? Ultimately, do we point to the deep hurts or desires that we hear and through those hurts or desires point to the living God who yearns for a world of justice, as the prophets of old did?

That last question is the prophetic part. If we're really listening, we don't just hear where the hurt is; we point to it to help the other person recognize this detail in his or her story. This is a detail from which healing may bloom.

It's helpful to return to the presupposition, whereby Ignatius invites us to correct lovingly those with whom we find fault. Love recognizes fear and worry and seeks to console. It doesn't pretend error is truth, but it does validate the concerns of the other and seeks a better, more inclusive path forward.

Those are the kinds of stories that are most successful. By engaging with the other through prophetic listening, we can create that common ground. We celebrate our common humanity. We can find a place from which to embark together. That place might be one of fear: I'm afraid for my family, myself, my future. Such fear cuts us off from one another and drives us inward. But if we do not recognize the fear, hurt, or trauma, we cannot build something together. We cannot weave a story large enough to encompass us all.

Recognizing and naming fear—or whatever emotion, concern, or value we identify through prophetic listening—is not an affirmation of the hurts and pain that a person may have inflicted. If fear led you into a brand of politics or a kind of ideology that hurt other people, those sins must still be confessed and repented for. Reconciliation requires that we right our relationships and seek justice. But if we do not allow our stories to seek out people, even people far removed from our experience, even people who have hurt us, and welcome them in, the healing cannot take place.

If our answer to the question *Whose am I?* sounds at all like, "Not theirs," then we can be certain we've got it wrong.

Let's turn to a specific example that will illustrate the temptation to resist careful listening. It's a temptation we all face, particularly when important matters are on the line. It's hard to engage in the slow work of prophetic listening when we'd much rather lead with the answer we've already convinced ourselves is right. But we need to ask ourselves, Is this story big enough to encompass all of us? Or have I made it too small and exclusive?

• • •

Catholic Relief Services was founded in 1943, a response by the Catholic community in the United States to the growing refugee crisis in Europe in the wake of World War II. As such, it was both unsettling and appropriate that as we prepared to celebrate CRS's seventy-fifth anniversary in 2018, the organization was again responding to a devastating refugee crisis. Providing humanitarian aid, advocating for just policies, and creating a culture of inclusion were just some of the relief efforts CRS was leading. We sought to share stories and bring in new support to bolster these efforts.

Social media, though, is an unkind place. And while I'm sure there were plenty of folks in 1943 who disagreed with the Catholic Church's involvement with refugee resettlement, they weren't able to air their displeasure through an onslaught of vulgar tweets and Facebook posts.

Our team had put together a brief video primer on Catholic social teaching as it pertained to migrants and refugees. The video featured interviews with leading Catholics, clergy and laity alike, who pointed to both Scripture and tradition to underline the importance of welcoming the stranger. Though the video was correct in its description of Church teaching and helpful in its distillation of centuries of Church thought, it still met with vocal criticism across our social media channels. And I doubt it changed any hearts or minds; it likely only reinforced those opinions already deeply held.

I remember a colleague shaking her head. "We should've known," she said. "Think of some Church teaching that you struggle with. Would a slick video and a recitation of Scripture change your mind?"

"I guess not," I admitted. Because the video already reinforced what I believed, I found it quite convincing. But seen through this perspective, I had to agree. It spoke to the head; it didn't move the heart.

As a result, we endeavored to make future content more reflective rather than descriptive, inviting people to pray through their own feelings and emotions rather than bludgeon them with how they were *supposed* to feel. Along the way, we were mindful to still make clear how we as a Catholic agency were responding—how we were welcoming the stranger—based on the Gospel values we professed.

I wouldn't recommend completely changing a humanitarian relief strategy because of a few uncharitable tweets. But it does provide a helpful case study in talking past one another. If we don't give space to the fears and concerns of others, even if we ourselves find those fears and concerns outrageous or offensive, then we won't change any hearts or minds through our stories, no matter how slick the production value.

Often, things that matter take time. We need a chance to reflect on these stories with which we disagree or that challenge our preconceived notions. We need time to weigh them against our own stories and sense of self.

This is particularly hard to do when real lives and livelihoods and futures are on the line. Can we invest in long-term storytelling that helps everyone see themselves in the narrative and builds and strengthens relationships? Or do we push through a narrower story that proves our point, gives us cover, and lets us move forward with our decision? Time is a luxury we don't always have.

Harder still, we have to take Ignatius's advice to heart and release any attachments we have to our own opinions or preferred way of doing things. What motivates you, what gets you out of bed in the morning, might be just that: motivational to *you*. It may serve as a starting place to build that story of us, but it might not be where you end up—and that's okay.

• • •

After that conversation on the T, I asked Alli how she came to decide to become a Catholic. No matter how much she loved the sacramentality of marriage, even that of the Eucharist, I assumed she hadn't arrived at that realization in the time since we left West Newton.

She looked at me shyly. "Well, all the things we talked about, some of the stuff you said, it had an impact, for sure. But it was my time in Ecuador. It was time spent with the other volunteers, seeing how their faith sustained and energized them. Seeing people's devotion to the Eucharist, the role it could play in the promotion of justice. That was when I realized it was something I wanted, too."

In the end, it was experiential and uniquely hers. It was the coming together of many stories: the stories of her close friends and fellow volunteers, the stories of the Ecuadorian people with whom she lived and worked, and it was my story too. Whatever role I played, it was one of many, a few seeds scattered in a field that contributed to her personal garden. My role was to accompany, and express my values and passions, and listen eagerly to hers.

Faith is a living thing. And in sharing this part of myself with Alli, it became incumbent on me to allow her to share that part of herself with me. Though that undergraduate version of myself may have desired to change others while remaining static, that's simply not possible. We can't spout facts and figures, point to texts and charts, and assume the world will bow to our great knowledge.

Our stories take us into the heart of another person; they demand that we reverence the shared humanity we find there. When we emerge, we shouldn't be the same person, though we may—and perhaps should—hold the same values and truths. But we make the story bigger; we give room for the other. Together, we continue forward.

An Exercise in Ignatian Storytelling

Opening Prayer

Pray for the grace to accompany others in the discovery of stories that speak truth, even when that truth makes you uncomfortable.

Prayer Text

And it happened that while they were conversing and debating, Jesus himself drew near and walked with them, but their eyes were prevented from recognizing him. He asked them, "What are you discussing as you walk along?" They stopped, looking downcast. One of them, named Cleopas, said to him in reply, "Are you the only visitor to Jerusalem who does not know of the things that have taken place there in these days?" And he replied to them, "What sort of things?" They said to him, "The things that happened to Jesus the Nazarene, who was a prophet mighty in deed and word before God and all the people, how our chief priests and rulers both handed him over to a sentence of death and crucified him. But we were hoping that he would be the one to redeem Israel; and besides all this, it is now the third day since this took place. Some women from our group, however, have astounded us: they were at the tomb early in the morning and did not find his body; they came back and reported that they had indeed seen a vision of angels who announced that he was alive. Then some of those with us went to the tomb and found things just as the women had described, but him they did not see." And he said to them, "Oh, how foolish you are! How slow of heart to believe all that the prophets spoke! Was it not necessary that the Messiah should suffer these things and enter into his glory?" Then beginning with Moses and all the prophets, he interpreted to them what referred to him in all the Scriptures. (Luke 24:15–27)

Reflection Exercise

- Place yourself in the prayer text, the road to Emmaus. Imagine yourself conversing with a close friend about something that has recently taken place, something about which you have strong views and opinions. Express your hurt and anger, your desired outcome. Your friend agrees.

- Then imagine a third person approaching, someone who holds different views from yours. He or she begins to explain how they came to hold these views. Who is this person? You feel yourself filling with emotions. What emotions do you feel, and what do you want to say in response? Is there a story big enough to hold both your opinions? What is at stake?

Conversation

Talk to God about the feelings that arose when praying through the imaginative exercise. Is it possible to find common ground with someone whose stances are so different? Ask God to help you understand these differing views, for the wisdom and the courage to pursue truth, and for the compassion needed to continue seeking common ground.

Journal

Make a list of values that you believe could serve as starting places for stories that welcome those with whom you disagree. How might those listeners respond? How would you hope they respond?

— 6 —

What We Act Against

Pop culture often reduces Catholic education to old nuns teaching Latin. But by the time I made it to high school in the early 2000s, nuns were few and far between in the Philadelphia archdiocesan school system, and Latin was so uncommon that it was introduced as an upper-class elective at the end of my high school career.

My Latin, as a result, leaves a bit to be desired. In fact, my Latin is limited, really, to the many phrases found within Ignatian spirituality such as *magis, Ad Maiorem Dei Gloriam*, and *agere contra*.

Why does this matter to us in our Ignatian storytelling? This question—*Whose am I?*—is all about identifying, building, and strengthening relationships. It's a recognition that we belong to one another; our stories are not told in a vacuum. Any path of self-acceptance and healing necessarily brings us into contact with others who desire that same healing and acceptance.

In the last chapter, we talked about our need to listen to the stories of others as a prerequisite to sharing our own stories. Practicing prophetic listening makes space for the discovery of shared values and thus allows us to heal wounds as a community and not only as individuals. We expand our stories to ensure there's space for all of us.

In this chapter, I invite you to reflect on the Ignatian principle *agere contra* as a way to actively carve out that interior space within yourself to not only listen to the stories of others but also to let them find a fertile, welcoming space within your own story and to see what you discover as a result. This chapter is an invitation to act against the impulse to build an impenetrable fortress around your heart—around your story of self—and instead make room for the stranger, the unexpected, and the surprising.

It's hard work. Too often, we're tempted to avoid coming too close to another person, emotionally and physically. Too much empathy, too much compassion leaves us vulnerable, and we may think that makes us weak. We are told to be strong, to leave nothing to chance, to prioritize our own good and the good of those we're closest to. If this is what we've been told to believe, then we may construct our story to reflect this reality. We may edit out or gloss over those parts where we fell short of this apparent goal. Yet the process of healing requires an honest assessment of our story.

Agere contra means "to act against." For Ignatius, this was a way of overcoming desolation. He wrote about it in the thirteenth annotation of the *Spiritual Exercises*, and his example is quite simple. It's hard to pray for an hour when in a spirit of desolation. The evil spirit might use that moment to slowly chip away at your relationship with God. Act against it. Commit to praying for an hour *and ten minutes*. In that way, you identify where the evil spirit might be wriggling into your life, and you overcome that devious wriggling by pushing against it through an intentional act that perhaps overcompensates. In that way, "one gets used not only to standing up to the adversary, but even to overthrowing him."[14]

What does *agere contra* have to do with storytelling? Here are some questions that might begin to put this spiritual principle into context: What must you act *against* in the stories you tell—stories about yourself, others, the world around you? What temptations do you face when telling stories? Must you act against the way you conceive your stories, in the language you use to tell them, in the way you present them to family, friends, colleagues?

For instance, my temptations arise around ego, my inflated sense of self. I must act against this and intentionally make space for others in my stories. It's necessary to reflect on myself, including those experiences and people that have contributed to making me who I am now. But when the self-reflection evolves into storytelling, my intent should go beyond my own benefit. If I told the story only for myself, then I could simply keep a diary.

Our story of self is told to our friends, children, neighbors, and colleagues, and it's told not only in words but in how we present ourselves, in how we offer suggestions and advice, and in how we simply exist in their presence. Who we imagine ourselves to be is projected from our words into reality, right in front of loved ones and strangers alike.

Shouldn't these stories, then, look to the needs of others, too? And what's preventing us from doing that? Whatever it is, that's what we need to act against.

It was a long road for me, realizing this, and it's a road that's ongoing. But let me take you along a key moment that might illuminate opportunities for your own practice of *agere contra*.

• • •

None of my luggage had arrived.

I watched a fellow traveler collect what was the final bag from my flight and suddenly realized that I was standing all alone at the baggage claim. Despite the late hour, the Queen Alia International Airport was busy, and I felt tired, anxious, and small. I trudged over to an attendant, who quickly discovered that the few Arabic words I knew were unhelpful. He confirmed what I suspected: I'd need to wait at least a day, likely two—and as it turned out, three—for my bag to catch up to me.

The delinquent bag was still in Canada. And I was in Amman, Jordan, with nothing but my camera, my laptop, some audio equipment, an extra shirt, and a *Star Wars* novel. And all this after a delay leaving Baltimore, an unexpected night in Toronto, a day—pleasant, though unplanned for—spent wandering Frankfurt, and a solid twenty-four hours lost from my intended time in Amman. Father Rob had already reworked our agenda twice.

I was in Amman for only a few days, spending time with Father Rob and the other Jesuits living in the Jesuit Center, Amman's Jesuit community. I would film activities at the Center, interview some of its members, record some reflections from the Jesuits, and then package the whole thing when I got back to the States. Some videos, a podcast episode, a written piece, maybe some social media stuff. I knew that the Center served a growing refugee community, and I felt sure that there would be a few good stories to share. I was interested to see what fruits Ignatian spirituality bore in a culture and a context far different from my own.

But now, I was on an ever-tightening timeline, perpetually tired with no hope of adjusting to the time change, and demanding far more from that one extra shirt than was fair to ask.

"So, I'll still get a chance to talk to some of the community members, right?" I asked.

"Absolutely," Father Rob said. "I've moved our appointments around, had to cancel some. But we should still be on track. I've invited a number of our community members to the Center tomorrow night. You can talk with them then."

"Great," I said. I could already feel myself fading as I listened to my Jesuit friend detail the week's agenda. We were sitting in the dim light of the Jesuit community's kitchen, sipping German beer, having already returned from the airport, my meager luggage deposited in my room. "I probably need two or three interviews, and that'll do the trick." My tired brain was wearily mapping out how and where to set up the makeshift studio and what I could jerry-rig as a stand-in for the tripod that was still flying over the Atlantic.

Rob nodded. "I'm sure you'll be able to get that from the folks who are coming. They're coming a long way, though, so you'll want to make sure you talk to everyone."

"Cool, cool. How far are they coming?"

"Some, maybe an hour. A lot of the refugees live just down the road, but some live a ways away. The bus route goes by the Center, so that's how many of them get here."

I gulped down my beer. "These folks are taking an hour-long bus ride just to see me?"

"Well, they love the Jesuit Center and want to share their stories."

"And how many did you say?"

Rob began to tick off on his fingers the different places where he'd advertised the session. "Fifty?"

"Fifty?" I'm not sure if the panic registered in my voice, but it definitely did in my eyebrows. They shot straight through my forehead.

I began to do some quick math. How many minutes were enough minutes to listen to a refugee's story on camera? Could I pair them up? Maybe some wouldn't want to share. Maybe they wouldn't show. But if even half of that group showed up and wanted to talk on camera and they averaged about ten minutes each . . . "Do you think they'll all want to share something?" I asked cautiously, coaxing my eyebrows back into place.

Rob shrugged. "There are a lot of powerful stories in that group."

I nodded. Was I about to turn away refugees? The dark irony was not lost on me: an American traveling to the Middle East to hear the stories of refugees, only to turn away the ones he didn't have time for. No, no. That wasn't an option. But I only needed a few minutes' worth of interviews, total. I wasn't even sure I had enough batteries to power all my equipment for that long. Had I packed enough memory cards in my carry-on luggage?

Despite the rain that night, Father Rob's prediction held: about fifty folks came, from Iraq, Somalia, Sudan, and more, as well as local Jordanians—all members of the Jesuit Center community. They ranged in age, but most were young adults, like me. They came from across the street and from the other side of town. And each came with a story.

When I entered the classroom in which they gathered, I still hadn't figured out what I was going to do about the interviews. How many could I realistically film? But when I walked in, saw that diverse crowd—all those people gathered because they believed in the community they had formed and the unique story that they alone carried—I knew I couldn't say no to anyone.

How inconvenient, really, was my lack of batteries and a spare shirt compared to the stories of women and men who had journeyed across international borders with only what they themselves could carry? What did it matter if I spent an hour or two or three more than I had originally planned when these young people had spent a year or two or ten more than they had hoped to, living as refugees in a land not their own? And how could I deem one story less important than another when each person sitting in front of me contained promise and potential that had been so abruptly interrupted?

I spent the better part of three hours quietly sitting behind my camera, listening. Each person's story was unique, but the parallels and general themes were unavoidable. Conflict, violence, and an overall feeling of being unsafe in their own homes and communities forced them onto the road. Many had seen people die, including close family members. An intolerance of diversity, a hatred for people seen as different, often led to the violence. For whatever reason, each of the people in front of me had been deemed *other*—an *other* religion, an *other* ethnic group—and forced to flee. I could almost hear the sounds of gunshots, screams, tears shed and lives lost echoing in the background of these tales.

Each story, too, told of dashed hopes: there were dreams of furthering education, advancing careers, and settling down, either in a new country altogether or, preferably, back in their homeland. The community that these young men and women had formed at the Jesuit Center was powerful, a place of hospitality and inclusion, where no one was "other" and all were welcome. Many of the individuals I heard from expressed their gratitude and detailed ways in which they themselves were giving back to the community, supporting their fellow refugees, and helping bring in others who were feeling adrift in a Jordanian society that could seem indifferent to their plight.

One man asked if I'd like to hear the song he'd written about his flight from Sudan. I merely nodded and adjusted the mic. The song was haunting, a lyrical history to preserve what he had experienced for future generations of Sudanese. Another Sudanese man told me the story of the violence he witnessed, his voice eerily matter-of-fact, subdued, and though I couldn't make out every word of his newly learned English, I couldn't unhear words like *killed* and *raped*.

It was numbing. Story after story, and I didn't know what to do. No one had made an obviously wrong choice or failed some cosmic test. These were just folks like me making their way in life until something forced them to make unimaginable decisions. And then, they did their best. But they wanted more. They dreamed of more. And many of them hoped that whatever I was doing with my hodgepodge collection of camera equipment and shoddy lights would help.

"I've never heard confessions," I said to one of the other Jesuits who lived in the community, after my night was done and my equipment safely recharging in my room. I was sipping at another German beer. "But I imagine it feels something like that."

Another of the few Latin words I know is *kenosis*. The recognition that God emptied Godself in becoming human, making room for the *other*—us—in the Christmas story, the Incarnation. We are all called to self-emptying, the removal of the messy self-stuff that gets in the way of our making room for the needs of another.

John the Baptist, speaking of Jesus, said it best: "He must increase; I must decrease" (John 3:30). How might that mantra serve us in our storytelling? How can we act against those tendencies in ourselves that get in the way of other people's stories? To act as though only our story matters?

I think back to my initial reaction when I heard that there might be fifty people in attendance in that little classroom in the Jesuit Center. Think of it: Fifty stories from women and men who have made courageous, heart-wrenching journeys just to find a bit of peace and security that so many of us take for granted. Fifty! Think of what it took for these individuals just to show up to the Jesuit Center that first time. To trust in community again. To actively believe in themselves and their dreams again, and to do so while collaborating for the common good.

And my first reaction had been to glance at my watch and check my battery power.

I was in Jordan to do a job. I knew what I needed to make myself successful: two or three interviews, stories that clearly spelled out the plight of refugees and illustrated how the Jesuits were working to help. I had already begun to put together a narrative in my mind, how I saw the story going. That story was very much in my own voice. I had allotted an appropriate amount of time to collect those stories and wanted to be sure I had an equally appropriate amount of time to rest.

Really, I would have been within my rights—professionally and personally—to cut those interviews off, to close up shop and pat myself on the back for a job well (enough) done. But just because I was within my rights doesn't mean I *was* right. What best served the relationships in that moment?

I'm no hero for sitting through nearly three hours of interviews. I'm no hero for recharging batteries, for listening quietly, for inviting folks in front of the camera and patiently nudging them to share their stories. The stories were not mine to tell. These stories did not need my voice, only my accompaniment and witness. I had to set aside my desire to tell the story in my own way.

This was a temptation of the ego. I did need to believe in my role there behind the camera, capturing the stories of young men and women. I did bring a certain set of skills to meet the needs of the moment.

But it was not my place to control the story. I didn't get to rest when I wanted to rest and film when I wanted to film. Inviting all those women and men to share their stories, intentionally recognizing that this might be *more* than I needed and yet *equal* to what the moment needed, was my practice of *agere contra*.

And perhaps next time, if I do the hard work of carving out space for others, when such a moment arises, my first instinct won't be to look at my watch and check my batteries. It might just be to welcome the stories and recognize that right in front of me is the answer to the question *Whose am I?*

An Exercise in Ignatian Storytelling

Opening Prayer

Pray for the grace to act against your prideful self-interest in listening to and sharing the stories of others.

Prayer Text

So they came to John and said to him, "Rabbi, the one who was with you across the Jordan, to whom you testified, here he is baptizing and everyone is coming to him." John answered and said, "No one can receive anything except what has been given him from heaven. You yourselves can testify that I said [that] I am not the Messiah, but that I was sent before him. The one who has the bride is the bridegroom; the best man, who stands and listens to him, rejoices greatly at the bridegroom's voice. So this joy of mine has been made complete. He must increase; I must decrease." (John 3:26–30)

Reflection Exercise

- When you tell or share a story, are you more concerned with your own appearance, reputation, or gains than with the true needs that the story points to? Are there temptations inherent in your storytelling that require you to *act against*?
- Enter the Gospel story above. If a group of your friends, colleagues, or even strangers tells you that another is doing similar work, do you respond as John the Baptist did, or differently?

Conversation

Talk to God about this mantra: *Others must increase; I must decrease.* What does God say? What images and experiences come up in prayer? God shows you your many gifts in your story and reminds you that those gifts are no more or less important than the many gifts manifested in the stories of others.

Journal

A common phrase in storytelling for social good is *Being a voice for the voiceless.* How might your storytelling lift up the others' voices while acting against the temptation to assume the role of being their voice? What tactics might you use? What situations should you try to be part of?

– 7 –

Story Standards

There's a line from Peter Jackson's 2001 film adaptation of J. R. R. Tolkien's *The Lord of the Rings: The Fellowship of the Ring* that's always stuck with me: "But they were, all of them, deceived, for another Ring was made."[15] Brief as this line is—and easily missed, as it's part of a longer prologue sequence—this sentence captures the stakes of the entire trilogy. Because the people of Middle Earth were deceived, because they didn't know the whole story, pain and suffering resulted.

On screen, we watch as rings of power are made and distributed to all the key players of Middle Earth: the Elves, the Dwarves, and the Race of Men. These rings represent influence, clout, prestige, and they bestow great power. We are led to believe they've been appropriately distributed. For whatever reason, these rings seem to reflect an agreed-upon order of things, how Middle Earth is organized and governed, how the inhabitants of Middle Earth make sense of their lives.

But they were all of them, deceived, for another Ring was made.

This deception is quite literal in *The Lord of the Rings*. Sauron made another ring, told no one about it, and amassed unimaginable amounts of power and influence as a result. The rest of Middle Earth went about their days assuming they understood how the various rings of power would influence their lives and livelihoods, but they were wrong. They didn't have all the information. They didn't know that the scales were tipped against them and had been from the start.

And thus, our heroic Hobbits appear on the scene to destroy the One Ring and make things right.

Stories help us see truth: in ourselves, our communities, and our world. But stories can also be used to conceal truths, intentionally and unintentionally. Stories can be used to maintain a status quo that's based on a lie. If we think we know about all the rings, then we tell stories that reflect that knowledge. But if we know there's *another* ring and that we're all potentially in danger as a result, then our stories should point that out.

Much in the same way that we may not realize the privileges we enjoy and how they affect the stories we tell about ourselves and others without doing some deep, personal reflection—as we discussed in earlier chapters—we may also fail to see the structural, cultural, and systemic injustices that make up the world around us. And if we fail to see those problems, we are doomed to repeat—even praise—them in our stories.

This chapter aims to provide a framework through which we can assess how larger, systemic issues are impacting our stories, and it offers a way to tell stories that act against these harmful systems. To do so, we'll reflect on the Two Standards, a pivotal meditation from Ignatius's *Spiritual Exercises*. Again, as we attempt to answer the question *Whose am I?* in our storytelling, we're invited deeper into the realities experienced by people different from ourselves.

• • •

Here's another example, taken from our own time and place: social media. I've taught courses in social media to undergraduate students, and I always begin the semester with an easy icebreaker: Tell me your name, what you study, and why you're in this class.

"I took this class because I want to be a YouTube star."

I remember doing a double take at the young man who had spoken. "Oh, really?" I replied, eyebrows raised. "Say more."

"Yeah. I've been working on my channel, building up my subscribers. You can make a lot of money on YouTube." He was a tall kid, loud, confident. He earned himself a few glares from around the room and perhaps a few admirers.

I nodded. "You can," I said, wondering if anything in my syllabus would help this aspiring YouTuber rake in his hoped-for millions.

For the majority of my students, the role social media can and should play in their professional and personal lives is assumed; it's taken for granted. The question isn't *if* they'll use it; it's *how*. How might I employ this tool for my personal gain? After all, no one takes a film-making course and questions the use of a camera. And yet what I try to get my students to grapple with over the fifteen or so weeks we're together is that social media isn't just a tool; it's an ecosystem. It's a cultural force. You don't just make use of social media in the same way you might make use of a camera. The camera can't use you back.

I remember one young woman from a different semester. She was quiet, sat near the back. And her answer on that first day had something to do with her Instagram account. She wanted to become an influencer, someone others looked to for advice, tips, and life hacks, and she saw Instagram as her ticket into that world. She had already amassed a number of followers, and her account looked clean, well-curated, and overall, professional.

This semester happened to kick off right after the Dolly Parton Meme Challenge went viral. Dolly Parton had created a square graphic, split into four parts. Each quadrant held a different image of Dolly. Underneath each image was written the name of a different social media platform: LinkedIn, Facebook, Tinder, or Instagram. Each picture of Dolly was distinct: some risqué, some professional, some fun and casual. They more or less matched the visual experience a user would expect to find on the social media platform listed beneath the image. The internet loved it, and countless users—famous and not so famous—spent the next few weeks making their own.

This became our topic on that first day of class. I asked my students to talk me through how they'd approach the Dolly Parton challenge.

Attending that class were aspiring influencers and brand managers and students who were already interning in the world of social media. These weren't amateurs.

"Facebook is where most of my family is," one said. "So I'd post a photo of me with my friends doing something I wouldn't worry about others seeing."

"Yeah," another student weighed in. "This is where I'd post stuff I'd *want* my mom to see."

Everyone laughed, agreeing.

"Now, Instagram," the first student continued, "that's where my friends are. That picture would be me being cute doing something cool. Like at a party or something. And Tinder—well, that photo would probably be—"

That's when I held up my hand. "Don't tell me anything I don't want to know," I said.

We went around discussing images, what was appropriate and what wasn't, depending on the platform in question. "So, do you have different identities on these different platforms?" I asked.

"Well, yeah," several students replied.

"Does that trouble you?"

"No," that first student chimed in. "That's just what you have to do. You have to act a little differently depending on what platform you're on."

"But who's the real you?" I pressed. "Where does the real you come into play?"

That was when the students averted their eyes, scratched their heads—thoughtfully, I guess—and hoped I wouldn't call on them. It was a good enough place as any to wrap up the first class.

Weeks later, I was grading the first assignment. It was a reflection paper, and students were tasked with thinking about their own relationship to social media. Did anything about it give them pause? What might they hope to work on? Were they happy with how they related to and through their social media channels? They were supposed to connect their thinking to something we'd discussed thus far in class.

The quiet girl who sat in the back and hoped to be an Instagram influencer wrote about the Dolly Parton Meme Challenge and our subsequent class discussion. Despite that well-curated Instagram feed—all those pretty pictures—she confessed to not really knowing who she was, who she was trying to represent on Instagram. She didn't know how to express her true self. She was under such pressure to share only pretty pictures, images that would convey the kind of life she was creating. It was all a fiction, though. The images on her feed didn't represent who she really was, and she didn't know how to process the feelings she had about the highly selective—and increasingly dishonest—process of becoming the influencer she thought she should be. She felt like she was losing sight of who she actually was and was becoming.

She committed herself to trying harder to be more honest with herself as the semester continued. But I don't know if she succeeded. Because the very nature of social media—the ecosystem so many of us are forced to play in—is powered by clicks and likes and comments, and if you fall out of favor, which can happen quickly and decisively, it can be all but impossible to claw your way back.

And so, if your identity, your income, and your relationships all depend on that kind of constant affirmation, constant recalibration to the changing whims and algorithms of the system, you can understand how a person might get lost. But you can also see how this system works just beyond our realm of understanding: Who changes those algorithms and why? What impact does it really have, and who does that impact serve?

This kind of systemic dependency is not limited to social media. Think of your own life. Think of the various systems of which you are a part: a belief system, an economic system, an education system, a media ecosystem. Are there assumptions that go unchallenged? Do you feel pushed to do things, to make decisions based on how the system works? Is that good for you, your family, your community?

Our stories are tied up in these systems. That's not inherently a bad thing. But, as in the case of my students, sometimes we lose ourselves in these systems; we forget who we *actually* are and what makes us unique.

One thing I never talk about in my communications classes is the downward mobility of Christ. There are several reasons for that, one being that I don't teach in the theology department of a Jesuit school, and another being that, well, it's kind of a bummer.

This downward mobility, reflected in the Gospel, speaks to how Jesus set his priorities. He's unconcerned with possessions or wealth; he doesn't even have a permanent home. He constantly pushes aside any honors or praise, often telling those recipients of his miracles to quiet down, hush up, say not a word of whatever healing powers have been revealed. And, of course, the great paradox of the Crucifixion: Jesus, the Son of God, exerts no power or influence over his captors but simply allows himself to be led to his death, exposing the cruel violence embedded in the structures of his society and embracing nonviolence, a tactic so often used by those who have no power, no force to call upon to save the day.

Poverty, rejection, and humility: these preferences mark the way of Christ. Saint Ignatius, in the *Spiritual Exercises*, even goes so far as to encourage us to pray for these things in our own lives, if God so wills it. Why? Not simply for some masochistic endeavor. Rather, if we are constantly prioritizing this downward trajectory, this antithetical path to all that the world so often calls us to, then we find ourselves more able to see through the fog, hear through all the noise, and pinpoint exactly where we are being tempted to go astray.

I wish I could talk about these things in my courses more frequently, because I think in many ways this downward path is the answer to what that quiet, would-be Instagram influencer was looking for: a radical rejection of the narrative that beckoned her forward, dangling likes and shares and retweets as though they were salvation itself.

Failing to recognize the role these systems play in our lives without our even realizing it means we can never truly become who we are called to be. Rather than heal, we haphazardly place Band-Aids.

I think, for example, of the young Black man living in fear of the criminal justice system in the United States, a fear that, as a white man, I simply do not share. The system looks differently at me than it does at him because of the centuries of prejudices and biases that have become so ingrained in our way of thinking that it takes work even to see them. The neighborhood I live in, the security net I rely on, the network of friends and colleagues I enjoy, and the way society sees me—all these things contribute to a system where I am seen very differently from my Black counterpart.

And yet, how do I extricate myself from this system? Is it even possible?

Our stories must grapple with these larger forces. We ask *why* things happen to us and our neighbors. And we point to that *why*, as we did in earlier chapters, as a way to understand what values—good, bad, and ugly—are being promoted in our society. As we find our way through our own stories, through the stories we share with and about others, we *must* point out these unseen forces and the impact they have. Is our society living up to the values it professes to hold dear? As we practice prophetic listening—as we *hear* the hurt experienced by others—we may find that we are pointing not just to the hurt, but through it to the systems in our society that continue to poke at the wound.

Saint Ignatius gives us a powerful reflective tool as we attempt to navigate these problematic systems, and it's built upon the downward mobility of Christ. At the end of the second week of his *Spiritual Exercises*, the retreatant is asked to meditate on what's called the Two Standards. Imagine a great battle between the forces of good and evil, of Christ and the Enemy. Imagine these two opposing forces represented by standards—flags, of a sort—upon the field of battle. You know which side you represent based upon which standard you stand beneath.

The standard of Christ is represented by those three virtues of downward mobility: poverty, rejection, and humility. Harsh words, but definitive ways in which to map the trajectory of our lives. Do we pursue only our own benefit, whether through ever-increasing wealth, status, praise, power, or privilege? Or do we set those things aside in favor of others and their needs? Do we allow those more self-centered things to get in our way, to guide our lives, to serve as the North Star of all our decision making? Or do we put Christ's mission of peace, justice, and reconciliation first and foremost?

The enemy's standard is the opposite of Christ's standard. It is represented by riches, honor, and pride. The one who stands beneath this standard seeks out wealth above all else, is obsessed with his or her reputation and status, and is always mindful of ways to gain power and influence over others.

We might simplify the difference in the Two Standards as this: Am I seeking my own benefit, or am I seeking that of others?

When it comes to storytelling, these questions are much the same. Do I tell stories to draw attention only to myself, my own work, my own accomplishments, or do I use my platform to shine a light on others, their needs, and their gifts? Do I manipulate and make use of others' voices, or do I allow them to speak for themselves? Do my stories challenge the status quo, or do I go along to get along, to maintain my comfortable position, income, and follower count?

In *The Fellowship of the Ring*, we experience the moment the wizard Gandalf has his worst fears confirmed: the ring in Frodo's possession *is* the One Ring, that great source of evil and suffering. I imagine Gandalf did some soul-searching in that moment. Here he'd known—or at least, suspected—that Bilbo, Frodo's uncle, had long had a ring of power in his possession. And Gandalf had done nothing about it. Here he was now, witnessing the slow, painful destruction of Middle Earth, and he'd had it within his power to stop it all along.

And now that the truth has been discovered, when Frodo tries to give Gandalf the ring, he refuses. He fears that he would succumb to the ring's power. He fears he would bring even more harm to Middle Earth. What he can do, though, is accompany Frodo on the path to the ring's destruction.

Perhaps that interpretation of Tolkien's work is incomplete, but in reflecting on Gandalf's character, I wonder if we can't see something of ourselves. We look out at the world, and we know things aren't quite right. Certainly not as God intended. We see racial injustice and the destruction of the environment. We see war and disease and hunger. We see corruption and the accumulation of unfettered power and wealth.

And yet, for so many of us, we get along just fine. Things could be better, sure, but things are good enough in our immediate circles. The larger systems haven't hurt us, not directly, not too much, at least. We turn a blind eye, as Gandalf did, to the rings in our midst.

If the outbreak and global spread of COVID-19 has taught us anything, it's that we're much more interconnected than we ever realized. And while our stories start in the deeply personal—who we are, what we believe to be important—they necessarily expand to include others, set against the backdrop of God's whole creation. If everything and everyone are connected, then how can we not point out those dangerous rings when we find them? How can we not, in our stories, highlight the fractures in the larger systems, the harm they will inevitably do?

The image I have in my mind is that of an otter covered in oil. Think of it: When you see a picture of an otter in oil, do you say, "I hope that otter gets cleaned up" and walk away? No, you're more curious than that. We ask how he got dirty—*why* is he covered in oil? Was there an oil spill? Are there other otters out there covered in oil? Have we found them? What about the other animals? What about that part of the ocean? How do we prevent this from happening again—and why did it happen in the first place? This otter's story is not a singular event; we find him in a larger context. And we want to know all the factors in play.

It's the same with us, with our stories, and with the people we meet.

The Two Standards help us know if we're on the right track.

If we set aside our desire for wealth, we may not concern ourselves with telling sensational stories that get a lot of clicks, a lot of likes, and a lot of commentary. Instead, we're free to tell those stories that need to be told: true stories. We aren't beholden to the preferences and priorities of those holding the purse strings. We uplift the voices at the heart of the story, unafraid if some may find those voices too challenging.

If we set aside our desire for honors, we free ourselves from the affirmation of the masses. We aren't beholden to the changing whims of our followers but can speak truth to power, can call people to be their best selves through our stories rather than settle for the lowest common denominator.

And if we set aside our pride, we won't be forced to create a fictional version of ourselves. The stories we share can be truthful, accurate representations of the joys and challenges of real life. We don't need to filter out images that are unflattering. We don't need to constantly check our phones to see if anyone has said something new about our work. And when we inevitably make a mistake, we can admit to our failure and move on. We can tell a new story.

Ultimately, this kind of storytelling is healing for all of us.

An Exercise in Ignatian Storytelling

Opening Prayer

Pray for the grace to clearly see systems and structures that perpetuate harmful narratives and to identify how you might contribute countercultural stories.

Prayer Text

Filled with the holy Spirit, Jesus returned from the Jordan and was led by the Spirit into the desert for forty days, to be tempted by the devil. He ate nothing during those days, and when they were over he was hungry. The devil said to him, "If you are the Son of God, command this stone to become bread." Jesus answered him, "It is written, 'One does not live by bread alone.'" Then he took him up and showed him all the kingdoms of the world in a single instant. The devil said to him, "I shall give to you all this power and their glory; for it has been handed over to me, and I may give it to whomever I wish. All this will be yours, if you worship me." Jesus said to him in reply, "It is written: 'You shall worship the Lord, your God, and him alone shall you serve.'" Then he led him to Jerusalem, made him stand on the parapet of the temple, and said to him, "If you are the Son of God, throw yourself down from here, for it is written: 'He will command his angels concerning you, to guard you,' and: 'With their hands they will support you, lest you dash your foot against a stone.'" Jesus said to him in reply, "It also says, 'You shall not put the Lord, your God, to the test.'" When the devil had finished every temptation, he departed from him for a time. (Luke 4:1–13)

Reflection Exercise

- Put yourself in the story. When the evil spirit comes to you, what are you tempted with? What riches? What source of power? What tugs at your ego?

- Think of the many systems of which you are a part: cultural, religious, economic, racial, etc. Are there aspects of these systems that pull you toward wealth, honors, and pride? Are there aspects that pull you toward poverty, rejection, and humility? How do you respond?

- As you consider your response to the previous question, begin to recognize the larger narratives at play, the stories you've been told and that you tell yourself, that you hear others tell to condone certain behaviors. What stories might you tell in response?

Conversation

Hear God whisper those words—*poverty*, *rejection*, and *humility*—in your heart. Share how they make your feel. Share, too, your struggle to make sense of Christ's standard in a world that hardly seems cut and dry, a world filled with nuance. How do you move forward! How do you avoid paralysis?

Journal

Write the words *poverty*, *rejection*, and *humility* on a piece of paper. Under each, note moments in your life story that exemplify the given word. How might these moments help others pursue Christ's downward path?

Part 2 Reprise
Answering "Whose Am I?"

COVID-19 shut down the world. And I—hunkered in my basement-turned-office—was focused on the people immediately in front of me: my pregnant wife and toddling daughter. The six weeks since I'd returned from Jordan felt akin to six years, and my mental and emotional capacity was suddenly near a breaking point. The plight of the young refugees I'd met in Amman quickly faded from view as I turned my attention to those in my family who were most at risk of contracting the disease.

Professionally, our team was working on putting together resources to help people pray through and reflect on the sudden, global shift. We were busy churning out new content daily: digital retreats, podcast interviews, videos, and more. Amidst the whirlwind of those first few weeks, an email popped into my inbox.

"Dear Eric," it began. "I hope you are safe and stay healthy with your family and loved ones. I am very sorry to see the sad news coming out of the States every day." It was from Aaden, a Somali refugee I'd met in Amman who had impressed me with his passion, his dreams, even his frustrations. (I've changed his name for privacy.) He went on to describe how the pandemic had affected his community and the refugees living in Jordan more broadly. He expressed his belief that God would bring us all through it, despite the challenges at hand. And he ended his message saying how he was in solidarity with me, sharing in the feelings and emotions he knew I must be wrestling with.

It was an overwhelming message. Here I was, so focused on my own family, my own work, my own safety. I never thought to reach out to him or any of the others at the Jesuit Center. My work had taken a turn, and we were in crisis mode. Jordan seemed a world away.

I stepped back from it, staring at that message. What could I say? What could I *do*? As frustrating as it was to be confined to my home, at least I had a home in which to be confined. As much as I would like to see a few additional faces each day—as much as I love looking at the faces of my wife and daughter!—at least I had close family by my side. I was privileged enough to have financial, physical, and emotional security and was only more or less inconvenienced. And yet, despite that comfortable position, it had not crossed my mind to reach out to Aaden.

When I had moved to answer the question *Whose am I?* in those initial weeks after the global shutdown, I had not thought big enough. My story was too small.

So I began to craft a response. And the Ignatian storytelling principles we've reviewed helped me see the direction this response should take.

First, prophetic listening. In detailing his own current predicament, Aaden had expressed solidarity with me and with others in the States suffering under the challenges presented by COVID-19. There was nothing in his story to correct or with which I disagreed; I was merely called to listen. In fact, his current experiences were nearly identical to what I was experiencing, to what many were experiencing across the United States. The difference, of course, was that he was living as a refugee.

That's where the opportunity emerged. How might his experience inspire others? Inform others? This wasn't a collection of facts or church teaching around the plight of refugees or our Gospel call to welcome them. This was a personal narrative that showed resilience, hope, and struggle, that illustrated similarities while also the stark, random differences that led his life to be quite different from my own.

This was an opportunity to be prophetic by pointing to something true and important.

Next, *agere contra*. There was a temptation to seize the credit and write the story myself. I could easily pull a few quotes from Aaden's email. This could have been a story about my moment of recognizing the differences between Aaden's situation and mine; it could have been about my own spiritual enlightenment. But I needed to act against this tendency. This wasn't my story to tell. More than that, I needed to elevate Aaden's voice and give him access to a platform he otherwise wouldn't have. I needed to be patient and humble in editing his work, in helping him craft an essay in a language that wasn't his first and for an audience with which he had no familiarity. This was important work—and it was *his* work. I was the supporting cast.

Finally, the Two Standards. It's not hard to see how this could have gone awry. Aaden's message would have made a great fundraising message. I could have easily made myself the hero of the story—or at least the story's primary voice. At worst, I could have just taken Aaden's kind message and turned it into a story, leaving him none the wiser, never inviting him into the storytelling process. Those, of course, are all quick paths to the enemy's standard: pride, honor, and riches.

Most important, there was a need to honestly reckon with the global system in place that favored me over Aaden as the storyteller, as the subject, as the hero. Aaden was still held hostage by an unjust, imbalanced series of refugee policies that kept him trapped in a land that was not his own while I sat comfortably at home. He was at best limited in his pursuit of his personal and professional dreams while I was, simply by receiving his email, improving both my personal and professional standing. The power imbalance was palpable, and I had to name that.

Helping him share his story on our website wasn't some heroic act that leveled the playing field and made up for years of oppression, violence, and injustice. But it was a small way in which his voice was liberated, his words found purchase in a new land and new ears. So I played my part but no more than that.

Whose am I? Religious traditions the world over have answered that question in much the same way: We belong to one another. We are our brothers' and our sisters' keepers. We are called to be the Good Samaritan while recognizing that we may just as easily find ourselves robbed and left for dead on the road. We are called to reconcile with one another and thus bring healing to the larger world.

Our stories must reflect this truth.

But more than *reflect* this truth, Ignatian storytelling demands that our stories *point the way* to a future where healing leads us to reconciliation and serves as our default setting. It's not enough to share examples; we must help one another imagine our way into that Promised Land.

— PART 3 —

WHO AM I CALLED TO BE?

Few sentences evoke such a degree of urgency in a person as this one: "My water just broke."

I scrambled out of bed, grasping at my phone and a light switch. "You're sure?" I called, pulling up the doctor's phone number. *Did I save? Did I save it as "doctor"? By last name? Oh, GOD, WHERE IS IT?!*

The reply was both simple and laced with irritation. "Yes."

We were only thirty-eight weeks into Alli's pregnancy and assumed we'd have a few more weeks to go. After all, your first always comes late, right? Wasn't that how this was supposed to work?

I got the doctor on the phone—I assume; it was three in the morning, and I was frenzied. Someone answered and said something. "Okay," I said. "Time to go." I reached for the hospital bag, reached for my wife. *Plenty of time. Just don't forget how to get there. No traffic this early in the morning.*

She nodded, thoughtful. "You know, I think we have a little bit of time. Why don't you clean the bathrooms real fast?"

"What?" I stammered. "The bath—We have to *go*."

"But our parents are coming down. We don't want dirty bathrooms. Just real fast."

"Uh—okay." I knew from the doctor, from my diligent listening at the doctor appointments, that Alli needed to get to the hospital as soon as her water broke. That's what the doctor had said; that's what

Alli had said. That's what my anxiety-ridden dreams had been saying for weeks.

But there was also something to be said about listening to your quite pregnant wife. So, I cleaned the bathrooms. Now it was 3:27 a.m. "Let's do it. I'll let our parents know once we're there and—"

"Just a quick snack," Alli replied, working her way down the stairs. "A little cereal. It's going to be a long day. We should get our sustenance while we can."

"We have snacks in the bag!" I was exasperated.

"It won't take long."

And so, there we sat, in silence, at the kitchen table, at 3:42 a.m.—just two days after that same table had hosted Thanksgiving—and gobbled down cereal. Well, I gobbled. Alli chewed and swallowed like a normal person fully in control of herself and not at all concerned that a *second* person was planning to emerge from that first person just a few long hours later.

An urgent situation—such as the imminent arrival of your firstborn—does not justify a chaotic response. As odd a request as cleaning the bathrooms was at three in the morning after your water has broken—and it *was* an odd request—the levelheadedness that Alli displayed was far more productive than my scramble. I got it together, but Alli's response is the kind we should all strive for in moments of great need.

It's tempting, I think, to respond to urgency with an equally powerful force. We get caught up in a culture of outrage and split-second decision making and lose ourselves rather than make a thoughtful return to our own values and experience, to better make sense of the moment. Often, that which is urgent surprises and shocks us, throws us off balance, and we fear we're not enough to meet the moment. Panic is only human, but it's not the only response.

Our Urgent Work

Harvard professor Marshall Ganz, in his public narrative framework, writes of the story of now.[16] That word—*now*—is meant to evoke a sense of urgency. Ganz talks about this moment in a story as a call to leadership; this is when the storyteller steps up and cries, "Follow me!" If done right, by this point the audience understands who the speaker is and what values are at stake—the story of self—and why the story relates to them, the audience—the story of us. The story of now is the moment for action. "This is what we're here for," the speaker may say. "This is why I've been telling this story."

This is the part of our stories that point us forward. This is where our own self-healing becomes an exercise in connection and reconciliation. Bruised and battered and imperfect as we may feel, we know our story, where we've been, and we accept the person we are now as a result. This moment is an opportunity to use our stories as beacons for others, pointing the way to what might yet be. Exploring our stories has helped us restore how we relate to the self. Reconciliation is an exercise in making right our relationships with others, restoring or reordering what is broken in our world.

This is the next step for our storytelling, and it's urgent work. It again asks us to imagine what could be and how we might get there. It's an invitation to others to share in this building of a new, bigger, more inclusive story. And it's slow work because it takes time to listen and understand and unite.

In some ways, we've already answered the question put forward by this final part of our storytelling journey: *Who am I called to be?* You're called to be a storyteller; you're called to tell your story, to live out of your story, and to walk alongside others as they do the same.

But if we think of ourselves as those leaders trying to tell a story of *now*, trying to meet the urgency of the moment, then we can see that there's still work to do. We're grappling with the signs of the times, attempting to read them, to understand where the need is greatest and how our individual gifts and experience might meet them.

To do so, we must use spiritual tools to recognize in our stories what can help others utilize their own stories to respond to the moment at hand. This is the opportunity for reconciliation—or, more precisely, when the long journey of reconciliation begins.

1. **First, we get in touch with our own restlessness.** We listen closely to what is stirring within our own stories and discern how best to use these holy whispers for good. In so doing, we identify ways in which we can guide others in directing their restlessness toward the common good.

2. **Next, we grapple with what it means to practice Ignatian indifference,** a way to hold all preferences lightly and yet remain resolute in our pursuit of healing and reconciliation. In truth, we've been dipping into Ignatian indifference this whole time. This practice of indifference is essential in channeling that holy restlessness. We're invited to consider ways in which we might help our listeners do the same.

3. **Finally, we balance contemplation and action,** recognizing that we need to bring the needs of the world into our prayer and the fruits of our prayer into the heart of the world's needs. We think not only of ourselves and this moment but of all those who will follow. We consider what our story will leave behind—and who might be left to tell it.

The hard truth is this: Though needs are urgent, solutions take time. The stories we tell are stories that must weave themselves into the imaginations of our listeners, inviting them into the long, hard work, the ongoing struggle of reconciliation.

— 8 —

Ignatian Restlessness

Think back to the last time you felt restless. How did that energy manifest in your life? Were your eyes wide open in the middle of the night, your mind bouncing from one uncompleted task, one potential disaster to the next? Were you pacing the halls of your house, your kitchen, your office, maybe just the alleyway out back? Were your hands looking for something to do, a project to seize upon, some nail to drive into some wall to hang some thing just to feel a sense of usefulness? Maybe it's just that pit in your stomach you feel on your way into work, the sense that you're not living up to your fullest potential.

Restlessness can sneak up on us: the sudden, phantom itch on the back of your neck that no amount of scratching seems to relieve. Or it can dawn on us slowly, building over time. But no matter how it appears, it always seems to demand something of us, if we want it to go away. We have to *do* something, take action *now*, if we're to recover any sense of peace in our self, our family, our work.

That temptation can lead us to make some rather poor choices: exploding in anger at our spouse, taking on a project we don't have the time or talent for, perhaps missing out on the real beauty of the moment because we've allowed ourselves to be distracted by our desire to *do* rather than *be*. Saint Ignatius cautions us not to make any major decisions when we're in such a state. Rather, we're invited to sink into the moment, good or bad, to better understand what is being asked of us, what we ourselves might actually need, where God's Spirit is at work.

Restlessness can lead to important breakthroughs in our story; we turn the page and begin a new chapter. But just because restlessness feels like an itch that needs immediate scratching, that doesn't mean we should rush the slow, steady work of crafting our story. Rather, this potentially holy restlessness awakens our inner self to something new, but we won't know what that something is if we don't learn how to pay attention. That's what this chapter aims to do: assemble the pieces of our restless selves into our life's vocation.

Witness to Beauty

Our trek to Machu Picchu began at an ungodly hour. We set out from Aguas Calientes, the small nearby town, to walk the switchback that could accommodate both the bleary-eyed hiker and the ideally more clear-eyed bus driver. Back and forth we walked in the early morning Peruvian chill, the sun still asleep in the mountains surrounding us, a heavy mist resting comfortably on traveler and pathway alike.

It was a beautiful sight, at least, what I could make out of it in the dim light. I climbed slowly out of the valley, out of darkness, mountains slowly taking form around me as rays of sun began to pierce the clouds and mist and shadows. There was a density to it, a weariness that the landscape seemed to shrug off sleepily as the minutes ticked by. That blanket of morning cloud shifted this way and that as the day yawned and stretched. Odd shadows skittered just out of view; something glittered, here, there.

It was one of those moments—one of those sacred spaces—where something inside me whispered, *Quick—take a picture.* My eyes darted about, desperately trying to assess the light, the shadows. A tinge of anxiety colored the corner of my mind: *What if I miss it?*

There's something so important, so unique, so spectacularly dazzling about this moment that if it's not captured . . . Well, that's it. Lost.

I was armed with an even-then antiquated digital camera. The year was 2012, and I was sporting something on a par with a high-end flip phone. My chances of capturing anything but blackness were slim. But nonetheless, *Take a picture*, the voice whispered. *You'll miss the moment.*

Never mind that I was *living* the moment.

But this is the urge that always tugs at me when I encounter raw and exquisite beauty in its natural habitat. Those places where you feel the presence of the divine. It's that holy restlessness. A coming face-to-face with something incredible. A desire, in that moment, to do more, to be more, to never let it go. It's that desire to go deeper, that nearly impossible balance of both being present to the moment and also open to what it might reveal.

When my eldest daughter, Elianna, was born some five years later, I was again reminded of this truth. That little baby shook her tiny fists at the flurry of iPhones that clouded her immediate air space, the metaphoric flash going off again and again. "You're just so cute!" my wife and I kept saying. "That outfit . . . That face . . . That pose . . . And you're growing so fast!" Like any new parents—or veteran parents, for that matter—we wanted to capture the moment.

Misty mountain or five-week-old daughter, the truth stands the same: There is beauty here. God's very self is here. It's so hard to simply be present, to stand and stare that beauty in the face without the filter of a lens mediating the awe-inspiring. How easy, smartphone in hand, to snap dozens of photos that will never travel beyond that small, scratched screen.

Then I feel as though I've done something meaningful with the moment. At least I've tried. I've recognized it for what it is and given it its holy due, even if I haven't quite understood what to make of it. I have a picture to prove it.

I think of that moment in Scripture—the Transfiguration—when Jesus invites his friends to the top of the mountain. There, they encounter something wonderful, beautiful, divine. God's very self. And Peter, so desperate to capture the moment, suggests building tents for all those present: he wants to hold on to that moment for as long as he can. And who could blame him? Among friends, he witnesses something truly unique, awesome in the most literal sense. Without a camera on site, tents were the next best thing.

My daughter hasn't stopped growing. Each day has its special moments, but they will pass into memory, perhaps even legend, and that is the proper order of things. No number of iPhone photos will stop that, though certainly a few will look good hung on the wall or safely tucked in an album.

The restlessness is there through it all, though. The details fade, but that holy restlessness, the holy desire to dig deeper into those moments, to learn all they have to teach, remains.

How might we harness that potential in our storytelling?

Saint Ignatius was always mindful of the inner workings of a person's spirit. Passions that arose, curiosities that awakened, desires that burned ever greater—these were all places, Ignatius claimed, where God was at work. Can we hear the voice of the divine speaking to us through our passions, curiosities, and desires, these very human qualities?

These are big words to toss around: *passions, curiosities, desires*. Rarely in the moment do I stop and think, *Oh—a passion has been awakened! I must write this down*. This is the work of the *examen*, of prayer and reflection and journaling. We discover these things over time.

Like a Butterfly

In the moment, we feel a spiritual tug. A need to do a double take. A fluttering in the gut. As I did trekking up the path to Machu Picchu. As I do when gazing upon my daughters. As Peter did on the mountain with Jesus. It's a recognition that God is here, the compass suddenly pointing true.

Ignatian spirituality invites us to sit with these stirrings, to discern if they are, in fact, of God—or if they are something else. We sense a call to something new, more, beyond ourselves. We experience it and want to bottle it up and keep it from moving about, upsetting our stomach and requiring that we keep chasing after it and second-guessing our decisions. If only we could nail down this restlessness and turn it instead into *rest*: simple and static and under our control. But holy restlessness is like a butterfly, flitting here and there, just out of reach, leading us ever onward.

Often, the Holy Spirit uses this restlessness to break through our walls, pass beyond our locked doors, and shake us out of complacency. Following that butterfly spirit, we discover new things about ourselves, where our unique gifts and talents and insights can be put at the service of the world's many needs. We often speak of this process as the discovery of our vocation: the way in which we put our unique self at the service of creation.

This awakening of some holy desire is an invitation from the divine to go deeper into the world. My heart stirs at the sight of my children; I enter more deeply into my vocation as a father. My heart breaks when I hear the story of a refugee denied a home; I enter more deeply into my vocation as a storyteller. My heart awakens at the light, salty breeze blowing in off the ocean; I enter more deeply into God's holy world—and commit myself to its protection and contemplation.

Warring Spirits of Consolation and Desolation

Restlessness is not always holy. I wake up many a night, restless because I'm unsure if I've turned off the stove or because I wonder if the shelf I recently installed will remain on the wall. Or I'm nagged by how little I accomplished the preceding day, which simply leads to worry about all that must be done the next day. This restlessness is a symptom of anxiety and does not bring us closer to God, let alone reveal our vocation. This restlessness may be a gift of the evil spirit and a sure sign of desolation.

Such restlessness points inward, to our own failings and worries and insecurities, and digs in. And yet how easy it is to mistake this restlessness as solely the working of the Good Spirit—particularly, in the dead of night.

And so, restlessness helps us navigate the warring spirits of consolation and desolation. We can think of restlessness as an insect. Is it a butterfly, riding the winds, beckoning us forward, beyond our current selves? Or is it a tick, burrowing under our skin, causing us to itch and sweat and tug at our own fleshy selves with nothing but disdain and discomfort? Clearly, we can detect which of these is of God and which is not.

Rarely, though, is the discernment of spirits so easily managed.

• • •

The sound was incredible. It was like thirty-seven drumlines had suddenly been conjured out of thin air, all to play the exact same note again and again and again. *Din. Din. Din. Din.* Faster, slower, faster, slower. Then—a flash of light, all necks whipping heads in the same direction. *Crash.* And the cymbals played.

The storm had come quickly, which I guess was a common occurrence at that time of year in the Philippines. Our little band of undergraduate do-gooders was gathered under a wide tin roof, which was keeping the would-be auditorium dry. Well, dry enough.

We had just completed our walk through the neighborhood, a literal tour of poverty, and the dark, imposing storm clouds summed up our mood. These families lived next to a dump site in the shadow of Manila, the nation's capital city.

We already knew that too many people throw away perfectly good items every single day. What was new, though, was meeting the men, women, and children who eked out a living picking those cast-off items out of the garbage. So common was this work—so devastatingly essential to survival—that a vast and winding array of tin homes had sprung up around the massive dump site, shelter for the workers and their families.

My nineteen-year-old eyes weren't quite wide enough to take it all in. Really, the handful of hours we'd allotted to visiting the place were bucketsful of hours short, and even then, what could be done? We were on an Ignatian "experiment," a Jesuit-sponsored service trip tacked on to that year's World Youth Day: a global gathering of Catholics young and old, plus the pope, in Australia.

The experiments were meant to provide spiritual fodder for our ongoing reflection. The encounters we had and the faces that haunted our memories would be brought into our communal prayer. We would bring those stories back with us to the States, to our college campus, and do something with them.

What? That remained to be seen. Certainly nothing on a par with the need of the moment. Dropped into the perilous existence of thousands of people, we took a hasty look around, shed a tear, shared a grimace, and jumped—quickly—back onto the bus, back onto the plane, back into the air-conditioned, well-stocked, adequately ventilated dorm rooms for just a bit of prayer, reflection, and consternation. After all, head space in a college student is reserved for books and parties and extracurriculars.

But back to that moment when the rain finally stopped and we could hear one another again. The children started running about, tugging at our clothes, smiling in spite of it all. And I remember pulling out my water bottle—a battered thing, something I knew could be replaced whenever I deemed it necessary, certainly refilled without much of a problem—and I squirted water at those dancing little kids. And they laughed and danced in and out of range as I splashed water here and there, a sad and sorry encore to the storm that had just passed. I could feel the weight of the eyes of the men and women—the residents of that little community—hanging on me, hanging on the frivolousness with which I played with their kids, the laughter, I assumed, that I pulled from those hungry little mouths.

I was so pleased with myself because it had been hard for me to connect with anyone during our few days in the Philippines, and the laughter and joy and fun that was so palpable in that moment made me feel that I'd done it; I'd arrived. My reason for coming to the Philippines had been realized, restlessness over.

It wasn't until I was back in the States, months and months of air-conditioned dorm living later, that it dawned on me that those heavy eyes watching my watery antics were likely seeing in my actions an ignorant and wasteful use of water. Nothing fun, nothing frivolous, but a serious, life-and-death matter. Their laughter probably sounded tinny and ironic.

That moment in the Philippines was very much a cannonball moment. Or perhaps more precisely, my slow realization of what my presence in the Philippines represented was. As I continued my undergraduate career, participated in more service trips, and spent my year in Bolivia, all these disparate scenes represented a string of metaphoric cannonball strikes.

And slowly I was forced to grapple with a hard truth: My time in these foreign places was helpful and formative to me, even if it was largely unhelpful and quickly forgotten by my hosts. What to make of such seemingly incompatible realities? The slow straightening out of my life wasn't worth the cost of who knows how many other lives in the Philippines, Nicaragua, Bolivia, and more. But the trajectory that those experiences set my life on led me to a concern for justice and peace and reconciliation. That's good, right? Even if not in time for those particular people that unknowingly, and perhaps unwittingly, helped me get there? Perhaps.

That was a humbling, challenging truth to wrestle with. I have yet to arrive at any satisfying answers. I'm still sorting through the wreckage the cannonball has left behind.

As unclear as next steps may be, the steps that led me to the cannonball strike are more obvious. And again, we turn to this idea of holy restlessness. That desire to go to the Philippines in the first place was nothing more than swatting at a persistent butterfly. How adventurous, I thought. How exciting. What stories I'll have to share!

Nothing in my calculation accounted for the real flesh-and-blood people at stake, though I had some vague sense of wanting to *help*. Nothing in those nineteen-year-old eyes saw the problematic nature of a white kid parachuting in to get a good look at poverty before airlifting out. I remember being apprehensive: this was by far the furthest I'd ever been from home. I remember being arrogant: surely there were better ways to organize this trip! I remember thinking that maybe this would give me some opportunity to figure out what international studies had to do with creative writing and why those were the two things I'd committed four years and several thousands of dollars to studying.

There was that little rumbling deep within urging me to go. The desires were ill-formed, incomplete, and misplaced, and yet the cannonball struck nonetheless, the damage done—for good and bad—and here I sit all these years later, wrestling with what was and what might still be. I think that's not a bad outcome. Because surely, tied up with it all is my vocation, an increasingly less-foggy plane of existence on which I can spot new and unique ways to apply those skills I have to share with the world. I look at myself, my mistakes, and wonder if I can rectify them. If I can make sense of them, can't I then do some good? Maybe.

It's worth noting: It was Ignatius's pride that put him in front of the cannonball—and countless lives were lost due to his refusal to surrender. Was it worth it? Without that cannonball strike, we wouldn't have the Society of Jesus or Ignatian spirituality, nor would we have any of the good (and occasional harm) that has blossomed as a result around the world. But, all those years ago, it's hard to imagine that the families and friends of those soldiers killed unnecessarily in Ignatius's company felt that the end result was worth it.

Desolation to consolation and back again, and yet that sense of restlessness can push us onward. We spend some time looking inward, yes, perhaps a bit too self-absorbed, until we see the wider world. We see how our own restless selves—incomplete and imperfect—might do some good for another person. That's the story of my time in the Philippines and beyond. That's how I come at the question *Who am I called to be?*

And this is the kind of story a keen eye for Ignatian restlessness can pull out of others, too. That restlessness inevitably leads us in front of the cannon, inevitably puts us within striking distance of God's holy cannonball, and when we're struck, out of that restlessness we can begin to piece together a new way of seeing ourselves and the world.

What does this look like in your life? As you've tried to scratch the itch of holy restlessness, have you come to a deeper knowledge of yourself and your relationship to others? Have you uncovered the source of that cannonball strike? When you pause to reflect on where that restless energy led you—or perhaps, where it didn't—do you see a larger truth about yourself? A more challenging question: Who might have been harmed by actions taken in response to that restlessness? Do you push on, nonetheless, in becoming the person God invites you to be, even if you made a few missteps along the way?

I think of these questions in regard to my time in the Philippines and the various ways I could have responded to my restless missteps, my grasping about for what God was calling me to do.

There's a version of me who comes back from the Philippines happy, with an interesting experience. There's a version of me who tucks those photos away, pulls the stories out at parties, and otherwise keeps my head down and my eyes focused on matters that I can readily see. There's a version of me who, despite winding up on the other side of the world due to a restless itch to *help* and *explore* and be *challenged*, comes back and assumes that itch has been scratched. A bucket-list item has been crossed off, and now I can move on to the next. Perhaps the cannon misfired.

There's a version of me, too, who, though struck by the cannonball, comes home eager for familiar comforts: warm showers and hot meals that are nonreliant on rice. I see that cannon strike as a near-death experience—woe is me!—and I consider myself lucky to have escaped it. It's not so much that I consider that itch scratched as I consider it a form of eczema best treated and removed. My attention turns inward; my story shrinks. My vocation, I reassess.

I'd guess that if we look closely at our own lives, at those feelings of restless wonder, a cannonball moment is lurking somewhere nearby. As storytellers and as those who accompany others in sharing their stories, I believe it is essential work to pair these feelings of restlessness with the uncomfortable cannon strike they often point to. If we believe, as Ignatius did, that these feelings of restlessness are the very whispers of God, then we must be courageous enough to follow them where they lead, to learn the hard lessons they point to, and to not let them shrivel up and die, whispers lost to the wind.

Sometimes we find ourselves able to create cannonball moments for others, as those campus ministers did for the lot of us undergraduates headed to the Philippines. It's more likely that our role is to help others—and to do the hard work ourselves—to connect that holy restlessness with those inevitable cannonball strikes *already present in our stories*. We have to weave those stories together. We have to help one another identify the cannonball strike—and piece together its potential repercussions.

This, I believe, is urgent work. Even cannon strikes fade from memory if not properly attended to.

• • •

Let's end where we began: beauty, and the restless wonder it evokes. We try to control it, contain it, but in the end, it escapes our grasp. We can do little more than stand back and scratch our heads in amazement—and that goes for scenic mountain passes and adorable, if slightly fussy, babies alike. It goes for painful moments, too: a soldier saint having his legs shattered only to discover God on his recovery bed, or a young undergraduate embarrassed to learn he may have offended an entire Filipino community. Restless wonder is still the result if we allow ourselves to be curious and humble and to shed the temptation of stubborn arrogance.

We might not be able to control where that restlessness leads us, but we can control how we respond, *if* we'll respond. Will we frantically snap a picture? Or can we allow what is good and beautiful to wash over us, usher us onward into the next chapter, ever more deeply into God's holy world?

If we choose the latter, we must make ourselves ready and available to see where the story leads us.

An Exercise in Ignatian Storytelling

Opening Prayer

Pray for the grace to embrace holy restlessness, wherever it leads, and to help others do the same.

Prayer Text

[Jesus said,] "Do not let your hearts be troubled. You have faith in God; have faith also in me. In my Father's house there are many dwelling places. If there were not, would I have told you that I am going to prepare a place for you? And if I go and prepare a place for you, I will come back again and take you to myself, so that where I am you also may be. Where [I] am going you know the way." Thomas said to him, "Master, we do not know where you are going; how can we know the way?" Jesus said to him, "I am the way and the truth and the life. No one comes to the Father except through me. If you know me, then you will also know my Father. From now on you do know him and have seen him." (John 14:1–7)

Reflection Exercise

- Consider this promise of Jesus: "There are many dwelling places." What might your dwelling place in God look like? How might you move from a sense of restless wonder to a resting in God's holy place?

- How might you help others—doubting, like the apostles—lean into their own holy restlessness, their own troubled hearts, as a way to discover their promised dwelling place in God?

Conversation

Hear these words of Jesus: "Do not let your hearts be troubled." And yet, your heart is troubled; your mind is full of so many things! Ask for God's help in sorting through your troubled heart to find the holy restlessness that is leading you onward.

Journal

Map out key moments that might connect your restless or troubled heart with the dwelling place God has set aside for you. How might your own vocation make that connection?

— 9 —

Ignatian Indifference

We ended the last chapter by admitting that we can't always control where restlessness leads us. We can't even control if we're feeling restless: it happens to us whether we like it or not. The results can be good, bad, or—perhaps worst of all—ignored.

This restlessness seizes our stories, taking them in directions we may not have anticipated or desired. How we respond is the key. Do you resist, suppressing those feelings until they explode in some other, unrelated way? Do you distract yourself, pretend the Spirit isn't whispering in your ear, urging you on to something new? Do you attempt to exert some sort of control, even though that may simply not be possible?

Do you inadvertently miss the signs pointing you to who you are meant to become?

This chapter builds on the idea of restlessness by introducing another Ignatian principle. The goal is to help us move beyond this restless state by recognizing it for what it is, learning what it has to offer, and then making ourselves available to whatever is needed next. Again, this question of who we are meant to be necessarily thrusts us into the world, into a web of relationships, and into the necessary work of muddling through life's daily challenges.

The principle? Ignatian indifference.

Indifference is a cold word, even if you put "Ignatian" in front of it. It leaves a bad taste in the mouth, the taste of apathy, uncaring, even bitterness. It evokes in the mind's eye the throwing up of hands, the shrugging of shoulders. *What can be done?* the indifferent one says. *I just don't care.*

Yet that operative word—*Ignatian*—makes the difference in *indifference*. *Ignatian* indifference points to something else entirely, the opposite of apathy. In fact, one cultivates this virtue of indifference because one cares *so much*. There is such a love, a fervor, a restlessness in the face of the world and all its needs and opportunities that it becomes nearly impossible to respond. There's just *so much to do*. Our passions are driving us every which way. So much can be done. That love for the world is boundless, exploding in all directions and, if not properly channeled, likely to wither in the sun. As explored in the previous chapter, our restlessness can lead us astray.

When we speak of Ignatian indifference, we must also speak of detachment. Detachment means we free ourselves from attachments, particularly unhelpful ones. We seek to free ourselves from anything that holds sway over us, over our actions or thoughts, and prevents us from being our authentic selves, the people God invites us to be. This might even mean setting aside things we like and enjoy when they cloud our judgment or prevent us from acting on behalf of the common good.

True detachment leads us to an interior freedom, the ability to act on behalf of God's people—advancing a world of justice, compassion, peace, no matter the cost or the outcome. This is the role of indifference: We are so enamored with God, God's people, and God's creation that we set aside our own selves and allow God to speak clearly to us, guiding us toward what is right and best, even when it's uncomfortable. We resist the temptation to put our thumb on the scale. We see clearly the invitation to do good and are able to recognize how we are uniquely called, because we set aside our ego and instead seek to discover how we can make a real impact on a particular need. We glimpse the importance of vocation.

The goal of this unique brand of indifference isn't a stronger pair of shoulders with which to shrug. It's an emptying of self, an unclenching of fists, a willingness to hold all things lightly to be ready and available to act in service of those most in need, where we might do the greatest good.

This doesn't mean we stand for nothing. Rather, this practice of Ignatian indifference helps us discern the greater good, and we do so by bringing our values, experiences, and insights to bear. Knowing who we are and who we belong to allows us to respond readily to who we are being called to become.

A Vocation Story

Throughout this book I've shared anecdotes and insights from my vocational discernment and my own ongoing story. My story reveals values and unique life experiences, passions and skill sets, and I've done my best to put those to good use. When you sit down to write out what you've done, where you've been, and what you hope to stand for, the patterns emerge all on their own. That life story begins to make some sense.

You've been doing that, too, along the way in this exploration of Ignatian storytelling. I hope those patterns are becoming ever clearer in your mind.

My process of discerning God at work in my story continues to reveal moments when I held too tightly to expectations and failed to see the larger vocational story unfolding around me. I went to Fairfield University to study international studies and believed that I was meant to have a job and live a life that looked like what I was reading about. I would live in Washington, DC, travel the world, attend important policy-making meetings, and make my mark on the world stage. Wasn't this what my restlessness was leading to? It's why I went to the Philippines, why I studied what I studied, why I decided to spend a year in Bolivia, hard as it was. I wanted to make the world a better place—and still do.

I want to share some key moments that highlight a *lack* of Ignatian indifference. Along the way I discovered that though my values may have been right and my restlessness may have been leading me *somewhere* good, though my experience of other people and their stories helped me better understand the urgency of the moment, I didn't respond in quite the right way. Perhaps you'll see yourself in these scenes. I hope you'll return to your own story and look anew at the Spirit at work.

The main lesson to take away, I think, is that our God is a God of surprises—and is often encountered in surprising places. If we lean in to those surprises, our story gets a lot more interesting.

Accept Disgrace Willingly

I sat in my childhood bedroom, on my childhood bed, reading. I had returned from Bolivia a few months earlier and was still in a state of uncertainty.

Sunday through Tuesday of each week, I was in Washington, DC. It was a cumbersome commute from the suburbs north of Philadelphia—many nights spent on friends' floors and in spare bedrooms—all for an unpaid internship at a social innovation nonprofit. From Wednesday through Friday, I cleaned a school at night and spent the day interning at a real estate investment trust so that I had money to buy the gas that would get my car back to DC Sunday night. And in those spare moments, I edited an online advocacy blog.

It was hard. Taxing. And I was tired all the time. Nothing I was doing felt quite right, like it was leading me where I needed to go. I was adding line after line to my résumé, but for what? It felt chaotic, directionless. I made just enough money to sustain the chaos. But that clear, obvious line of thinking that had brought me through my undergraduate career and into the *campos* of Bolivia had become a squiggle.

Accept disgrace willingly.

That line struck me. It still does, years later. It's a blunt, concise summation of Christ's Standard; I'm confident Ignatius would agree. Rejection, humility, poverty: all these things appear as disgraces to the human eye. Those words echo John the Baptist's sentiment toward Jesus: "He must increase; I must decrease" (John 3:30). Indeed, this sense of surrendering self is bound up in the Christian understanding of the Incarnation—Jesus' coming down to earth, *kenosis*—in which God emptied Godself, "taking the form of a slave, coming in human likeness, and found in human appearance" (Philippians 2:7).

Accepting the disgrace of rejection, humility, and poverty is unavoidable in the Christian life and key to Ignatian spirituality. But the text that instructed me to *accept disgrace willingly* was no Christian text. This line is found in the thirteenth chapter of the *Dao De Jing*, a text attributed to Lau Tzu who was living and writing in China in the sixth century *before* Christ. This short work is foundational to Daoism, a Chinese philosophical tradition that shares many principles with religious and philosophical traditions the world over.

So, there I sat, in my childhood bedroom, wrestling with what seemed to be a series of wrong turns, a Daoist text in my hands.

"I believe it's vital," my spiritual director once said, "to the inner life of all those who are serious about their Christian faith to learn about and from an Eastern religion." Coming from a context and culture and history so vastly different from what formed our Western religious traditions—specifically, Judaism, Christianity, and

Islam—an encounter with Eastern traditions meant an encounter with the Spirit at work in a different way.

When my spiritual director pointed me toward Eastern thought, I was in my second year of undergraduate studies and deep into the course that would introduce me to Daoism. I didn't appreciate it at the time, but this Jesuit advice was very much in keeping with Jesuit history, one full of missionaries who traveled throughout Asia, learning from and discovering God at work in the people and traditions they encountered. I often wonder if missionaries like Francis Xavier and Matteo Ricci were surprised to find God waiting for them among such supposedly godless people.

Three years later, I sat on my childhood bed, returning to a text I'd examined only through an academic lens. This time, though, I took it to prayer; I invited God to speak to me through these ancient words rooted in a time, place, and culture quite different from mine.

And the Spirit spoke: *Accept disgrace willingly.*

I am not a Daoist. But approaching this text with reverence and awe, allowing myself the freedom to find God there rather than put up barriers around where God was *supposed* to be was pivotal to my prayer during those many months of post-Bolivia limbo. I was and am a Christian, able to dig deeper into my faith tradition and my experience of God's Spirit, by occasionally passing through a Daoist door. I was given a new vocabulary with which to speak of God's activity in my life.

Here I found God speaking to me in a new way yet saying something familiar, anchored in my understanding of God at work. These words of the *Dao De Jing* gave me a new perspective on those words of John the Baptist, of Jesus, and of Saint Ignatius; they reaffirmed them. I returned to Christianity's sacred texts with renewed insight and eagerness, a new openness to God's word.

This posture was important at that moment in my life. Bolivia had represented for me an intense experiment in faith: a Catholic organization, a Catholic mission, a deepening of Catholic faith. And I couldn't shake the feeling that it had all gone wrong. God had been present, of course, but I couldn't help feeling that the particular brand of faith with which I'd gone to Bolivia, which I'd trusted to see me through, had somehow fallen short. Now, back in the States, I was trying to find my way again.

Perhaps those many months of tiring work, an exhausting commute, and little to show for them were something to be accepted: a disgrace to my eyes but something more to God. Whatever was going on, it was mine to wrestle with. Resisting, feeling bad for myself, and lamenting what could have been would get me nowhere. Though it was a mantra plucked from a Daoist text, it was a Christian principle that I repeated again and again over the subsequent weeks, months, now years.

Accept disgrace willingly. And then, the end of that short chapter: *Surrender yourself humbly; then you can be trusted to care for all things. Love the world as your own self; then you can truly care for all things.*[17] Words Jesus might have uttered.

Accept Simplicity Willingly

Let's do a thought exercise. What does it mean to you to live simply? Living within your means? A smaller house, only one car, enough clothes to get you through the week and no more? You don't waste food, own only one jacket, get your books from the library? Yes, that can all be true.

Simple living doesn't simply mean not having stuff; it also means not allowing stuff to have control over you. I think, for example, of how I should react when my daughter loses pieces of my *Star Wars* LEGOs; then I think of how I *actually* react. Then I realize that my

Star Wars LEGOs have a bit of control over me. I probably shouldn't freak out when pieces wind up under the couch.

This is an unhealthy attachment. Not debilitating, but not great. Detachment, then, is the obvious solution.

But simplicity isn't just about *things*. Simple living must also manifest itself in our ideas.

Think of a meeting room filled with colleagues about to launch a new initiative. You're invited to that meeting, excited to share a new idea. You stand and present the idea, and it's affirmed. People like it. You're eager for—and seemingly due—praise. It was your idea, after all. You should be credited, rewarded. But others take that idea and begin to bounce it around, using what you offered as a starting point. By the meeting's end, your original idea has grown and evolved so much that it's hardly recognizable as yours. You leave the meeting frustrated, maybe even angry. *That was my idea*, you think. *And they took it.*

Lost is the fact that your idea proved to be the seed that blossomed into something greater. But you were so fixated on credit, on having your name attached, that you lost sight of what the whole goal of the meeting was. You lost sight of what your hypothetical idea was meant to accomplish. You were irrationally *attached* to that idea.

A Franciscan priest shared this thought exercise with me at a conference once. "And that," the Franciscan concluded, "is a mindset that prevents simplicity. You are owned by something; you are not living freely. What started off well enough ultimately paralyzed you; you were unable to act in that meeting. You became so attached to what *was* that you were unable to support what was *becoming*. The common good suffered as a result."

In the First Principle and Foundation, the true preface of the *Spiritual Exercises*, Saint Ignatius makes a bold claim: Human beings are made "to praise, reverence, and serve God." All other things, Ignatius says, are given to us to help us achieve our end: God. "To do this,"

Ignatius writes, "we need to make ourselves indifferent to all created things. . . . We should not want health more than illness, wealth more than poverty, fame more than disgrace."[18]

Our values help us set our sight on what matters and guide our actions in bringing about that goodness. Ignatian indifference helps us keep that goodness in view. It helps us approach life open to new ideas and opinions, available to new directions, and unattached to matters that may inadvertently pull us down.

This is the approach that brought me to the *Dao De Jing* and allowed me to learn something new about the values I already held dear. They remained my goal. Openness to a new approach only served to better illuminate them.

But this story also reminds me that I have to *let go* of not only my *Star Wars* LEGOs but also my inflated sense of self. My story is my own, but I place it at the service of others.

Accept God's Invitation Willingly

The promise I made to myself upon accepting an unpaid internship with a six-and-a-half-hour round-trip commute was that I would maximize my time in the nation's capital. I fully expected to leave with a full-time job.

"Tell me more about what kinds of programs we support," I said to my new supervisor. We were walking briskly through the streets of DC, headed to lunch. It was January and cold, and my hands were tucked snuggly in my coat pockets.

"We run campaigns that connect entrepreneurs and philanthropists around social good," went the reply, or something to that effect. I wasn't really listening. I was teeing up my next response.

"It sounds like we could really add a religious dimension," I said. "Connect faith-based actors, that sort of thing." That's what I believed to be my niche. I could talk the faith-based game. I could connect it to peace building and justice work and add tremendous value. That's what my ego said.

My supervisor nodded. Smiled. She saw an eager intern, someone who didn't grasp the complexities of grants and mission statements and organizational budgets, someone who was desperate for a job and stable income. Who could blame her?

"Religion can be a powerful force for good," she said.

Or something like that. Who can remember? All I know is that I could tell I wasn't going to get any guarantees on that first day. I was already feeling deflated. My idea was so good, my value so obvious. *How can she not see it?*

I don't quite remember what I was hired to do as an intern; I worked at a large nonprofit with a start-up feel, and everyone was doing a little bit of everything.

"Take a look at these résumés," one of the managers said a few days into the internship. "See if you see anyone who might be good for the graphic-design position. I'll forward you some emails."

Am I qualified for that? I thought. It seemed a cruel task to make an intern—so apparently ineffective at writing his own cover letters—review the cover letters and résumés of would-be hires.

"Do you know anything about audio editing?" another colleague asked. A different day, a different request. "We have an interview we're hoping to make into a podcast, but no one has time to listen to the whole thing."

No, I knew nothing about audio editing. But I could learn—and I did. *But what good is this?*

Competent execution of odd jobs led to a steadier stream of tasks with more interesting outcomes. "Do you feel comfortable writing a series about our new campaign? It'd be nine parts. And you'd be ghost-writing for someone."

Hard to say no, though ghostwriting hardly felt like the way to get my name out there. Nonetheless, I sat at the little desk in the common space and reviewed the campaign components.

None of this appeared to be getting me closer to my goal, my dream job, as foggy as that end appeared. But still, I imagined myself working at some international nonprofit or the government or a think tank. I imagined myself as some great peacemaker, a scholar. I scanned various law schools, trying to figure out what international law was and what it took to work in it. Surely, someone interested in religion and peace could contribute, no?

I held so tightly to this as-yet-unknown image of myself that I barely registered the skills I was honing, the fruits of the present moment. *Picture your perfect job, and work backward from there*, people told me. But I couldn't figure out what that job was, and even if I did, was I already too late? I was on a professional tightrope, with little room for error, let alone exploration. My frustration grew.

I took off a few days from my various jobs to visit Alli in Boston. It was March, still cold, and the future was still clouded—for both of us.

"Well, what jobs *have* you been applying to?"

"Just stuff in DC. Think tanks, government work, nonprofits, that sort of thing."

She shook her head. "Maybe you have to expand your search. Is there anything else you could look at?"

I shrugged. "There are a lot of church jobs. But I don't want to work a church job." That feeling of betrayal by all things Catholic while in Bolivia still clung to me, and I was determined to put some space between me and the institutions I felt had failed me.

"A church job? What does that even mean?"

"I don't know. Like, Catholic stuff. At a parish or a Catholic nonprofit. But I want to expand beyond that. I don't want to get pigeonholed."

"Is there a particular job you're thinking about?"

"I saw something at Catholic Relief Services. But I don't think that's for me. That's not what I'm envisioning for myself."

• • •

My story shows that restlessness can be a good thing, a force of passion and desire and eagerness to be harnessed and channeled into a vocational enterprise. But we must make ourselves available to what that vocation winds up being—even if it's not what we anticipated or planned for. Otherwise, all that restlessness can leave us spinning in circles, not unlike how I felt balancing an array of random odd jobs. I was so determined to focus my energies in one direction that I nearly missed the whisperings of the Spirit all around me, nudging me in a different one.

Management skills, audio editing, writing: these are all seeds of intern experiences that bore fruit and continue to bear fruit in my current professional life. When I finally stepped back and allowed additional possibilities to surface, that perhaps focusing on writing and storytelling *was* what I was called to do, and that my own faith might be worth applying in a professional way, a career path slowly became clear.

But our storytelling does more than chart a career path. Fostering Ignatian indifference in both how we uncover our stories and how we share them with others, can help our listeners hold different possibilities lightly. When our stories reflect our own wrestling with different options, our availability to understand and make sense of those possibilities, we make room for others to do the same.

This isn't just a theoretical exercise. Problems that matter in our world today, problems that affect real people—migrants; refugees;

individuals struggling with homelessness and hunger; communities oppressed by violence; victims of racism, sexism, and homophobia—have not been solved because there are strong opinions on *both* sides of the equation. Staking our flag in the sand and barreling toward it might make for a compelling tweet or a motivational news segment, but it rarely brings about the consensus needed to change hearts and minds.

I am not proposing that Ignatian indifference means giving equal weight to sheltering the homeless and keeping folks out on the streets, or equal weight to perpetuating systemic racism and working to be antiracist. We've already spent time digging into our values, those things that are good and true and just, and my values say that everyone deserves a home and that racism should not be tolerated. But fostering an attitude of Ignatian indifference makes us more available to new and innovative solutions and perhaps unexpected collaborators. We find ourselves freer to pursue that ultimate good, trusting both in what we know to be right and just *and* in God's Spirit of surprises.

Our stories must be big enough to encourage this kind of thinking and opportunity. It's possible for me to listen to and grapple with the fear a family member expresses regarding refugees coming into our country while also steadfastly pointing to the need to protect the dignity of life and the rights of all people. But I might be required to hold my opinions lightly; I might be required to hear things that make me uncomfortable. In doing this, I can begin to bridge the gap between my values and the real world, my values and those of another. I might be surprised by the results.

This is the slow work of God. And it can be frustrating in the face of such urgent needs. But life's paths are winding, and more often than not, it feels as though we are stuck on the scenic route.

• • •

Even after accepting the job at Catholic Relief Services, I kept my eye on some theoretical peace-building position. I poured over graduate programs that would fill my evenings with coursework on religion, peace, and the ethical intersection of the two. I saw myself as a peace builder, a scholar, some heroic negotiator, even though my personal history seemed to tell a slightly different story.

As I went about my daily tasks at CRS and discovered the impact, small as it may have been, my writing was having on real people in real time, I found myself being tugged in a new direction. I began to reflect on my passion for writing and storytelling and the experiences I'd had that proved the case. My daily work began to reveal gaps in my storytelling abilities; I knew nothing of photography or filmmaking, for example. And I also found myself exploring academic programs that focused more on media and communications than peace building or religion, though I could begin to envision how all these things could work together.

I still wanted to do something worthwhile that promoted the common good, that served the intersection of faith and justice. Perhaps what that was, though, was different from what I'd expected it to be.

Was this an opportunity to *accept disgrace willingly*? Perhaps that's too harsh a term, but bound up in this question of reexamining my assumptions, holding my opinions and intentions lightly, and treading humbly, was a need to detach from the image of myself I'd held so tightly. That persona, perhaps, was being rejected, but the person who might emerge would be better for it.

"If you had to guess what kind of graduate program I would be interested in, what would you say?" I was in the car with a colleague. We were on the way to a meeting. She knew me and my work, but not deeply. It was exactly the kind of opinion I needed.

She glanced over from the driver's seat. "Well," she said with a shrug. "I guess something in communications? You seem to have a knack there. You're not a bad writer. Is that what you're thinking?"

"It wasn't," I admitted. "But it is now."

Who in your life might provide you with such an opinion? As you continue to journey through your own story, are you open and available to being surprised by some unforeseen plot twist?

I wasn't. But that didn't matter. It seems to be working out anyway.

An Exercise in Ignatian Storytelling

Opening Prayer

Pray for the grace to cultivate indifference in your storytelling in order to be more available to the true needs of others.

Prayer Text

Accept disgrace willingly.
Accept misfortune as the human condition.
What do you mean by "Accept disgrace willingly"?
Accept being unimportant.
Do not be concerned with loss and gain.
This is called "accepting disgrace willingly."
What do you mean by "Accept misfortune as the human condition"?
Misfortune comes from having a body.
Without a body, how could there be misfortune?
Surrender yourself humbly; then you can be trusted to care for all things.
Love the world as your own self; then you can truly care for all things.[19]

Reflection Exercise

- Select one line from the prayer text above to be a personal mantra for your day. As you return to it, consider the past stories and experiences it brings to mind.

- How might this idea of accepting disgrace willingly enable you to respond to the urgent needs of the world?

Conversation

Talk to God about the experience of praying with a religious text that is not your own. How does it make you feel? How is God speaking to you through it? What new insight into your own religious tradition does it offer?

Journal

- Write down moments from your story that illustrate the practice of Ignatian indifference.

- Returning to earlier exercises, identify in these anecdotes where your values were at play. How did Ignatian indifference influence you?

- Finally, consider how sharing these insights with others might help them recognize their need for Ignatian indifference.

— 10 —

A Legacy of Contemplation and Action

You know the feeling you get when you come to the end of a good book or turn off the TV after watching the series finale of one of your favorite shows? Even the most satisfying ending leaves you sad, reflective, restless. You know the story has to end, but still, you want more. Why? Because that story meant something to you; it affected you in some profound way. And now, you don't get to look forward to the next chapter or episode. It's on you now; *you* have to figure out what that story means to you and how it might influence your life from now on. It lives in your imagination, shifting from story to memory.

For my three-year-old daughter, the answer is easy: she pretends she's the warrior princess and saves her little sister from all sorts of peril. The story lives on in her everyday experiences. But for those of us for whom it's no longer appropriate to run through the halls swinging toy lightsabers, it's not so easy to express a story's legacy.

A good story rattles about in our head for weeks, months, years, maybe a lifetime. We tell our colleagues about it; we encourage our friends to read or watch it. We quote it and reference it and do all we can to remember it and bring it back into our lives.

If we do that with fictional stories, how much more do we—*must* we—do it with real stories, our stories and the stories of those we love?

Ignatian spirituality invites us to be contemplatives in action, to observe the nitty-gritty details of our lives prayerfully, carefully, intentionally—and then act on what our observation reveals. In so doing, I believe our stories leave a legacy, bread crumbs back to the people we are in this moment and also a challenge for those who will find those bread crumbs in the future.

I hope you have come to accept that your story is intrinsically, uniquely valuable. You have something to teach other people; you have something worth leaving to those who will come after you.

In this final chapter, I want to paint a picture for you of what the legacy might look like, what it could be, from my own encounter with legacies of two people who lived as contemplatives in action. Reflecting on their stories has taught me something about where Ignatian storytelling can lead us.

A Less Visible Road

Conventional wisdom suggests that you not let your grandmother sleep on the floor when she comes to visit, particularly if she's had to cross state lines and climb three flights of stairs to reach the solitary room you've rented in an old Baltimore rowhome. Conventional, though, is not how I'd describe my grandmother.

"It'll be good for my back," she claimed. Who was I to suggest otherwise? Her back wasn't great, far as I could tell, and my little twin mattress probably wasn't going to help any. I had blankets and pillows and things, and she was comfortable enough. At least, that's what she said.

It was Ma's first time to visit me in Baltimore. She was an avid hiker and a world traveler; Baltimore was certainly not a new destination for her, nor an exotic one. But she was eager to see what my new life in the city looked like. "We'll have time to talk," she'd said happily. "I can hear about your new job."

It had been a long time since she'd climbed any mountains, though she'd been to Egypt only a few years earlier. My grandfather, gone some ten years at that point, had not been as eager a traveler, and so she'd clocked many miles after his passing. A way to work through grief, perhaps, in the sands of the desert, the winding roads of ancient towns, and in the company of rare and wonderful wildlife from the African Sahara to the beaches of the Galapagos.

Nonetheless, her trip to Baltimore was a real challenge. She arrived within that first year of my moving to the city, before I was married and had a real place of my own, before any kids, before I even had a particularly reliable car. Ma didn't care what we did, though; she just wanted to see what my current situation looked like. A day in the life, if you will. And so, she laced up her shoes, and I led her down that one route I knew in the city: from Charles Village south through the Inner Harbor and Harbor East and eventually into Fell's Point, where I believe we got some ice cream.

We walked on smooth pavement and hazardous cobblestones and brick and grass and over bridges and past water and through dodgier neighborhoods and past surprisingly expensive shops. I can't imagine any of it was good for her back. But she never complained.

"I haven't been to Baltimore in ages," she said, her stride not quite keeping pace with mine, her head of gray bobbing at about my shoulder. "It's all very pleasant."

"Well," I replied, "where we're walking, anyway."

She nodded, knowingly. "It's so good what you do, though, helping people. So important."

I'm not quite sure if, under any degree of pressure, Ma would have ever been able to articulate what it was I did. Could I have, myself? But she knew that in some way, somewhere down the supply chain of human decency, I was doing *something* that benefitted *someone*—and that I also got to write and travel.

"Where are you going next?" she'd ask. "And are you going to take me? I don't take up much room in the suitcase." A chuckle. It was true; she was a slight woman who, if folding a person were possible, would fit snugly in a carry-on.

That night I remember sitting side by side on my little twin bed after we'd eaten dinner and pushed the soles of our shoes just as far as they could go. We sat there talking about faith and God and the world.

"I'm wearing the cross you brought me," she said. It was a ritual; she was *always* wearing a cross I brought her, but she wanted to make sure I'd noticed. On my first trip overseas, I'd picked up something simple from Assisi. She'd thought that was just fine. I'd done my best to carry on the tradition, finding some little cross she could put around her neck and think about the places I'd been, places she'd likely never get to.

I nodded, smiled. "There's a prayer I've been saying," I said, "by Thomas Merton."

"How's it go?"

"My Lord God, I have no idea where I am going. I do not see the road ahead of me. . . ." I went on from there, ending with "you will never leave me to face my perils alone."[20] I paused, looked at her. She was nodding, brow furrowed. I said, "It speaks to me of discernment, trusting in God, even in the uncertainty. I think that's where I am these days."

She didn't smile, just looked at me, lips pursed together thoughtfully. "I don't know that I like that prayer," she said. "God seems so distant. Not very friendly. That's not how I know God."

Ma was a committed Lutheran, and I was a committed Catholic, and for years we had agreed to disagree on things of faith. We'd challenged one another, pushed and parried. No amount of academic catechesis could placate the hurt she felt when we told her she couldn't go to communion, couldn't receive the Eucharist. "God welcomes all," she'd say. And I agreed, yet my attempted explanation as to why she had to remain behind in the cold, lonely pew seemed to suggest otherwise.

But this prayer? I wasn't sure why she didn't like it. Merton's prayer always makes me think of how *close* God is, how invested God is in our lives.

But I simply nodded that night, concealing my surprise. Perhaps the words had struck too close to home for her. The road doesn't become any more visible, it seems, as we age.

Family Rituals

My other grandmother, Nana, had a faith that was different though no less fierce. She attended Eucharistic Adoration every Monday—pulling my grandfather along with her—and was a eucharistic minister for nearly thirty years. When I became a eucharistic minister at my home parish—still only a high school student fumbling about for a way to fit in, some meaning in my teenage years—she bought me a pyx, the holy little Tupperware container used to carry the body of Christ. She gave all us cousins Miraculous Medals, I assume at birth; I can't remember not having it. And when I got older and wanted something simpler, she and my grandfather bought me a golden chain with a simple cross, a less explicit reveal of my Catholicism but no less significant to its nourishment.

All that to say, when I opened their gift to me on my confirmation and saw the hookah and some fresh tobacco, my grandparents had already established their Catholic credentials in my eyes, if not in the confused eyes of the others who had gathered to celebrate my third and final sacrament of initiation.

Nana had an intense devotion to the Blessed Mother, to Mary, and the way she talked about her, you'd think they hung out on the weekends, that when my grandmother slipped into the other room, it was to quickly call the Mother of God to check in, see how things were going, exchange brownie recipes.

My brother graduated from college in May, traditionally the month of Mary, and the whole family was making the trip to Nashville to celebrate. My grandmothers were not ones to miss an event in the life of their grandchildren, and so Nana piled into the van my dad had rented to make the trek halfway across the country.

"You know, every year the Catholic Daughters choose someone to crown the Blessed Mother in the annual May Procession," Nana had said to my mom a few weeks earlier. "And you know who they asked this time?"

"You? That's great, Mom!"

"Well," Nana continued, in that dry, matter-of-fact tone. "I had to turn them down. It's more important that I'm in Nashville, anyway." My mother was not pleased to hear the sadness in my grandmother's voice.

And so, that's how it came to be that my brother, my mom, my grandmother, and I stood before a statue of Mary, the mother of God, in a seemingly random Catholic church in Nashville, Tennessee, with a flower my mom had brought from Pennsylvania for my grandmother to lay before the Blessed Mother. We were silent, though I think one of us ended up humming *Ave Maria*.

Nana's eyes welled with tears all through that Mass. "She thinks of her own mother on days like these," my mom whispered. "It's kind of nice, though, that the Blessed Mother reminds her of her own."

Ritual applies to more than religion, and for Nana, food was a ritual. Food and family. And how often the two went together: All of us, gathered there in the small home, where my grandparents raised my mom and uncle. Our names handwritten across the tops of stockings hung over and around and placed alongside the fireplace (there were a lot of names) or a bowl full of chocolate heart candies placed in the center of the living room table or the tiny charcoal grill they'd gotten for free at the casino out back, burgers and hot dogs sizzling.

On Easter, Nana would make us all special Italian cookies, carefully crafted to resemble various Easter critters—bunnies, ducks, chicks—and decorated meticulously with sprinkles by my grandfather's own hand. As we aged, moved out, took up new residences, each mailing address would receive a batch of said cookies, packaged in more aluminum foil than one can expect to find in a single roll.

Her cooking was all-consuming. There weren't enough tables in her house to hold all the Thanksgiving plates. The salad, for example, was always forgotten, covered in plastic wrap and banished to a side table below eyesight and elbow height and not the main course anyway. A turkey *and* a ham, and both prepped days in advance, samples from the strategic frozen meat reserve. And if her brother was coming, no matter what the occasion, there was always some tripe, an Italian specialty too frequently placed next to the meatballs, and I could never tell the two meats apart until it was too late, swamped in red sauce as they were.

"Nana, how are you?"

"My heart. Number one. How are you?"

"We're going to be passing by the house. Coming back from a wedding. You and Pop around?"

"Of course!" I could hear the wheels turning in her voice. "I have some lunch meat; we'll make sandwiches. Some pickles. I think I have some ice cream sandwiches in the freezer."

I could see Alli's face out of the corner of my eye. Lunch meat, hardly my favorite, was definitely not within a vegetarian's diet. "That's alright, Nana. We're okay. And Alli doesn't eat lunch meat, remember? Vegetarian."

"I'll take care of it," she said. We arrived, and there she was at the front door, hands on her hips, apron on, smiling. She'd summoned an entirely different meal out of her pantry. We didn't even get the pickles. But that's just how it was: you visited, you ate, you were happy.

By contrast, my other grandma, Ma, was not a chef. Cooking was not her strength. She had a hard time even ordering for delivery without a bit of guidance. "But what *kind* of pie do you want? We had chocolate last year. Is that alright?"

But she always wanted to help, always wanted to *do* something. Be productive. Always wanted us at her home, one far too big for an elderly widow to manage, that home where she definitely should not have been mowing the lawn on her own, where there was always some tree to uproot or pipe to fix or new carpeting to install. But she wanted us there so we could be together as a family.

I came late to the understanding that place and gathering are important. That it's a grace and a privilege to welcome loved ones over the threshold of your own sacred space. I didn't understand years ago, but I did it anyway. That's how we ended up adding a new tradition: Thanksgiving breakfast, our annual omelets, a food so exotic to Ma's typical breakfast of cottage cheese that she eagerly watched over us in her kitchen as the onions sizzled. She wanted to help and, if she couldn't do that, she at least wanted to be where the action was.

"What a bunch of a chefs! I'm so glad you're here."

A Familiar Story Relived

I've heard the Gospel story of Martha and Mary so often that I roll my eyes whenever it's part of the Sunday readings. This old story? *Mary the hero; Martha the worrywart.* As a rather anxious person myself—your typical type A; a poster boy for a One on the Enneagram—my heart goes out to Martha. She's just trying to keep the house in order. They are hosting Jesus, after all.

I was with Alli in Boston, attending Mass at the church where she would later be confirmed, and this was the reading on deck. Cue eye roll.

The priest stood up, and you could tell he was feeling the way I was feeling. Maybe he even looked me in the eye, gave me a knowing smile. Probably not. But he got to the pulpit and said, essentially, Listen, we all know this one; we all know that Martha is the active one and Mary the contemplative, and we know that, in fact, the Christian life requires both contemplation and action.

"I'm not going to tell you anything new," he said. "So, let's just try it out instead; let's try to be contemplatives in action. Let's listen to the reading quietly, again, together. Let's *do* what the reading is talking about. Let's see what happens."

And so we did. He read the Gospel again. We observed a moment of silence. And that was that. I don't remember any lightning strikes that day, but ever since, this is the moment I return to whenever that reading comes to mind. Whenever I consider the contemplative and active people in my life. Whenever I pause to reflect on what it means to do both, to live both fully, differently, pointing to something more with the simple deeds of your life.

At the outset of this Ignatian storytelling journey, we reflected on what it means to engage in imaginative prayer, to enter *into* a sacred story to learn a bit about ourselves, who God is inviting us to become, and where we might fall short. In some ways, that priest was inviting us to bring that Gospel story into our *actual* lives, to consider it, weigh it, see how it measured up against reality. That day, I didn't imagine myself playing the role of Martha or Mary or Jesus; I imagined those roles of Martha, Mary, and Jesus superimposed on my life and the people in it.

To contemplate something means we're really taking it all in: the good, the bad, the ugly. It means we stand vulnerable and raw and allow what is true and real to wash over us. We don't shrink back from the uncomfortable; we immerse ourselves in it. We allow tears to fall or laughter to rise or a quivery lip to have its way. We welcome what makes life, *life*: from that first kiss after the wedding vows are said to the devastation wrought on a lifetime of work in the wake of a hurricane. The beautiful sunsets but also the bloated bellies of starved children.

In these moments of contemplation, we encounter God. But God isn't just pointing something out, making sure we don't miss something on a road trip or feel that pinch of pity that makes us fumble for our wallets. This is God revealing to us the signs of the times, what matters now, what is urgent and needed and necessary. How we might respond. How God is already at work.

And then, we act. We go out into that world of need and beauty and wonder and devastation, and we roll up our sleeves. We get to work. We do our best while admitting to our own necessary limitations. And then we bring those experiences back into our prayer, into our contemplation.

It's cyclical, like a fountain at a mini golf course. The water spills out, bubbles over, and then churns back in. And it all happens again and again and again no matter how many colorful balls get stuck floating in the mess.

Martha and Mary are just two sides of the same coin. What matters, I think, is that they entertained God, they welcomed the sacred into their home, dared the divine to come close. Both pointed to the Christ; both—in all their anxiety and calm and contemplation and action—looked in the face of that which is holy and reverenced it with their very selves.

They were friends of Jesus, no? One wonders how they met, what sustained that friendship, how often they saw one another. What did they do after Jesus left the house that day? What was it they then felt called to do? Certainly they didn't sit about contemplating the empty space Jesus had inhabited; they *did* something: visited neighbors, went for a walk, put a roast in the oven. They appear only a few times in Scripture, but obviously their lives expanded past those days and events.

Contemplation in Action

Contemplation in action means living in a way that is mindful of both the beauty and the urgency of the moment. We have only so many moments before our stories end. What will they mean once we're gone?

There was one Thanksgiving that we spent in the hospital. Nana's kidneys were failing. Things weren't looking good. We gathered around her bedside—no ham, no turkey, not even salad. Just family. Not the holiday we'd expected.

She recovered, as well as could be hoped for, but we knew those kidneys were going to be trouble. And so they were. Some years later, Nana was in the hospital again in the middle of the global COVID-19 pandemic, newly moved with my grandfather from their home in New Jersey to a much more manageable place near my parents.

"God's not going to take me just yet," Nana said to me. She was sitting on the hospital bed, looking perfectly herself: calm, well-dressed, and slightly irritated at the poor-quality hospital food. "I'm going to have some more time with your grandfather, get him set up in the new apartment."

I nodded. "That's good to hear." I had rushed up from Baltimore, masked, with pockets full of hand sanitizer. Nana's self-diagnosis was not at all in keeping with what the medical team had told us. "What makes you think that?"

"I've got Mary right here on my shoulder," she said. "But it won't be long now, I don't think. I feel scared but also peaceful. I just want your grandfather to be okay."

"We'll look after him," I said. "Try to hang in there though. Elianna still wants to watch *Beauty and the Beast* with you."

Nana smiled. She loved that movie, loved the songs.

Then we prayed the *Magnificat*, that great prayer of Mary's by which she proclaims that God will lift up the lowly and bring about justice for all. It was one of Nana's favorites.

A few weeks later, she suffered a stroke. This was a cruel turn of events because, hardly a year before, she had helped my grandfather recover from a stroke of his own. Had managed to pull him from the driver's seat of the car, get the car parked on the side of the highway, take the wheel herself. Eighty-eight years old, and no question in any of our minds she saved both their lives.

• • •

"I just feel so helpless," Ma said. My dad and I were visiting her at the nursing home where she had recently moved, also to be closer to my parents. She'd started out in independent living, but one accident after another had reduced her independence dramatically. Now, we sat on opposite sides of a plexiglass wall, all three of us masked. "I wish I could do something to help her."

Ma was visibly upset about Nana's stroke, the fact that she was back in that same hospital, lying on a bed, unable to communicate with any of us, life slowly slipping away. "I wish there was something you could do, too, Ma," I said. My dad had already encouraged her to pray.

But Ma had spent many years of her life as a Stephen Minister; she was the one who went to others in their moments of grief and pain. To be stuck behind a plexiglass wall, unable to move about without a walker—her hiking days long gone—unable even to hold her head up on her own, it was killing her. There was nothing any of us could say.

Her eyes brightened, though, when Alli arrived with Ma's two great-granddaughters. And that had to be enough.

It was late October when Nana passed away. We'd had our one last family gathering before her stroke; Elianna had danced with Nana to "Be Our Guest." Thanksgiving that year was solemn, different. We called Ma on Zoom, but she wasn't herself. All we knew was that she was glad to see us. The next day, we learned she'd contracted COVID-19, and not a month later, she died of it. We managed one last Zoom call; we couldn't visit her in person. But they'd said she was doing well, on the road to recovery, and then she wasn't. None of this went the way things are supposed to go.

I remember the last conversation I had with her. She had still been feisty, curious, herself. Unable to work her phone, ultimately hanging up on me, but not before she'd told me how proud she was of me, of my girls.

A Quiet, Powerful Legacy

The sudden loss of both of my grandmothers mere months apart left me in a somber, reflective state. The death of a loved one leaves a gaping hole, as any of us who have struggled through loss can attest. My grandmothers had always been there. They'd always been available for a quick phone call, a short visit, summer vacations, and family holidays. They'd been present at important moments in my life from my early childhood on the West Coast, far from family, to the early days of my own fatherhood, raising my own family.

But more than additional guests at my wedding or birthday cards in the mail, I came to realize—perhaps too late—that my grandmothers were my connection to the past. To my past. To a past in which my family story took root and grew and blossomed. And as I raise my own children, as I reflect on the relationships they have with my own parents, their grandparents, I realize that I only knew a very small part of who my grandmothers were. Thirty-two years, more or less. I rummage through boxes of their old things, their photos and jewelry and family heirlooms, and guess at what it all might mean.

As I find myself drawn to travel and adventure, I find myself wondering what Ma would think and do, where she would go. I know we shared a common itch to get out and see more, to dream big dreams and tackle them as best we could. What of her story am I called to live out? Am I being invited to write a new chapter in her story? We are all part of God's great story, after all. Perhaps the book is never finished; we just write new chapters. Our stories are all part of the same saga.

I sometimes imagine Nana in the kitchen, quietly, happily preparing something that will bring people together. I hear her voice when I grow frustrated in the daily struggles of parenting: encouraging me, cautioning me, reprimanding me for messing up my daughter's hair. And I see her in the Blessed Mother, Mary, mother of God. It's as though Mary and I share an old friend. My own prayer life feels to be an extension of Nana's.

"What did you two used to do together?" I might ask Mary. And Mary might smile, remembering days of Nana's past that predate me by decades.

We talk a lot about the communion of saints in the Catholic tradition. It's merely this: The stories we stand upon and live out of and continue to make sense of, stories of saints and sinners and grandmothers, stories that formed us and form us and give us something both to hold on to and to strive for.

The stories aren't easy. We see things we missed, moments we missed, topics we never asked about. We look back at the raw and the brutal and the heartbreaking. We stare at it, hard as it might be. But this grappling with stories, with legacies we're left to carry and make sense of, this is how contemplation turns to action.

Whose legacy are you carrying? Have you taken the time to sit with it, look it over, let it soak into your very self?

Telling the Whole Truth

When *Star Wars: The Last Jedi* was released, the fan base was split over the depiction of Luke Skywalker. He wasn't the mystical warrior people wanted him to be. He was just a tired, disillusioned old man who was trying to make sense of both the life in front of him and the life he'd already lived. Mistakes he'd made. Roads not traveled. I think it was too real for people. Fantasy is supposed to transport you to other worlds, not make you take a long, hard look at your own. Or is it?

What does any of this have to do with our Ignatian storytelling? Practicing contemplation in action in our stories means telling the truth, the hard truth, bringing people into deeper contact with where God is at work, even if it's uncomfortable and sad and heartbreaking. If we don't do that, if we don't sit with and be present to the brutal raw reality in front of us, if our stories fail in that regard, then we'll never be able to recognize that which is urgent in our world. We will be too tempted to shrink back and avert our eyes. Our stories will be incomplete. And the end will surprise us, leaving us wishing we'd done more.

Our stories are our legacy. They're what we pass down, what others will pass down on our behalf. They represent who we were, what we stood for, who we tried to be for ourselves and for others. And those stories, then, outlast us. They do the reconciling work after we're gone.

How we tell our stories matters. Are we honest? Or will we be remembered as someone who didn't care to separate fact from fiction? Are we focused solely on ourselves and what we may gain through our stories? Or do we allow the spotlight of our storytelling to fall on others? Do we tell our stories in a way that challenges the status quo, that pushes for justice and reconciliation? Or do we go along to get along?

The Ignatian spiritual storytelling principles we've been reflecting on should guide you in your approach to how you tell your story. Seek out shared values that inspire and motivate, and discern how best to articulate them. Sink into daily details that allow others to recognize the importance of the seemingly mundane. Always be available to accompany others in their storytelling, offering a gentle ear and prophetic voice. Act against the temptation to make yourself the sole hero and be mindful of the temptation to riches, power, and honor. Don't be afraid to allow yourself to feel a little restless, but don't give in to easy answers. Cultivate that spirit of indifference and recognize your story as part of the Great Story.

What do you want others to remember about your story? More important, why?

I have a small statue of the Infant Jesus of Prague that belonged to Nana. It reminds me of her faith, a faith that always invited you in, into her home, to feel safe and comfortable and to be refreshed. I have a small statue of a lighthouse, one of the many Ma collected. It points outward, searching, looking for more, looking for adventure, looking to meet the need where it may be found.

A holy statue and a lighthouse. Contemplation and action. Symbols that hold stories.

What symbols might hold your story? What would you give to others to contemplate, to inspire action?

An Exercise in Ignatian Storytelling

Opening Prayer

Pray for the grace to see clearly the urgent needs present in your story and in your world.

Prayer Text

As they continued their journey he entered a village where a woman whose name was Martha welcomed him. She had a sister named Mary [who] sat beside the Lord at his feet listening to him speak. Martha, burdened with much serving, came to him and said, "Lord, do you not care that my sister has left me by myself to do the serving? Tell her to help me." The Lord said to her in reply, "Martha, Martha, you are anxious and worried about many things. There is need of only one thing. Mary has chosen the better part and it will not be taken from her." (Luke 10:38–42)

Reflection Exercise

- Put yourself in the story. Who are you? Who are you not? What do you learn as a result?
- Consider Jesus' words: "There is need of only one thing." What is that thing? How might you know it, truly, and respond accordingly?

Conversation

Spend time listening to God describe the great story of creation. Consider all you see and hear. Then ask God how you might contribute now, in this moment, to meet the most urgent need.

Journal

What of your story do you hope continues to inspire others once you're gone? Who are those others? What inspiration might they seek?

Part 3 Reprise
Answering "Who Am I Called to Be?"

For a long time, I believed that if one was to consider oneself a peace builder, that meant that peace building paid the bills. I took courses and read books on peace building and all it entailed—justice, reconciliation, dialogue—and looked for ways in which I could put those principles into professional practice. At CRS I found myself surrounded by impressive colleagues, many of whom had the word *peace* in their titles. I had one particularly inspirational colleague from the Philippines who once told me how blessed she considered herself to be able to say that her vocation so perfectly overlapped with her professional career.

I saw it, too, the impact that this peace work could have: an imperfect though hopeful peace in Bosnia-Herzegovina, sustained in no small part by the ongoing struggles of religious leaders; the slow, steady rebuilding of Sierra Leone in the wake of civil war; the incredible resilience and determination of the Vietnamese people, only a few decades after our own sad history of war. In my own streets of Baltimore, a city representative of so much of the country, the work of peaceful antiracist activists and demonstrators moved leaders to act for justice. Even my own faith tradition and formation revolved around the stories of martyrs, brave women and men who fought oppression with nonviolence and who paid the ultimate price.

A Spiritual Mandate for All

How I wanted to lay claim to that word—*peace*—in my own job description, in some meaningful way in my own life! Its impact was undeniable.

For my final project in graduate school, I challenged myself to pray with a spiritual book on peace. I turned to Henri Nouwen's text *Peacework*, a posthumous publication that collected that prolific Dutch priest's writings on peace spirituality. As I worked my way through the text, this truth became increasingly obvious: Peace may be a job description for some, but it's a spiritual mandate for all. And here I was, putting off the important work of peace building because I had mistakenly assumed I'd not yet gotten the job.

As we near the end of our extended reflection on Ignatian storytelling, as we wrestle with this question *Who am I called to be?* we reexamine the purpose of our storytelling. Are we prepared to transition from self-healing to societal reconciliation? We seek to restore right relationships, to do the hard, slow work of justice, to promote the common good for all while lifting up those so often forgotten. If we are Ignatian storytellers, this is what our stories seek to accomplish.

And so, the answer to that question suddenly becomes quite simple. Who am I called to be? I'm called to be a peacemaker. I'm called to reconcile. And my storytelling—my accompaniment of others in discovering and sharing their own stories—is how I live into that vocation.

In this final application of the principles we've reflected upon, apply these images to your own life. Where is God inviting you to share your story? How might your story become a story of peace?

Where God's Peace Is Needed

As we assess restlessness in our world and in ourselves, we might think of it as an indicator of where God's peace is needed. Something new is at work; something is bubbling up just beneath the surface. Civil unrest or anxiety over a big life decision: either of these is a pivotal moment when the full story must be told. It's our task to listen closely to the voices that such restlessness reveals. Are they of God, or are they something else? Does this restlessness point to a new experience of God, a deepening encounter with God's vision for humanity—a vision of justice, compassion, and equality—or not? Identifying restlessness calls our attention to where the Spirit is at work.

Practicing Ignatian indifference gives us the fortitude to see peace as the ultimate goal. We remove our egos from the story and focus on how the Spirit is inviting us to achieve God's peace. This might mean giving up some of our privileges, comforts, and preferred or expected ways of doing things. Without that attitude of indifference, we're tempted to cling to such things, even if it keeps us from the peaceful outcome, that hoped-for reconciliation we desire. We see our story as part of God's great story; we expand the picture, making room for others and their needs.

Finally, we contemplate the real people, problems, hopes, and challenges of the moment, and then we act. We constantly refresh ourselves with the stories we hear from others, the struggles and joys and workings of the Spirit. We bring those lessons to God and take our own lessons from God to others. We have no choice but to affirm what is real, what is right in front of us—the suffering and the rejoicing—and to act. Together, we weave a story that reflects God's desire for our human family, a dream that is built from one generation to the next upon justice, for peace through reconciliation.

As we do this work, this spiritual practice of storytelling, we will recognize our stories as scraps of the collective memory, brought together to make real what might otherwise be ignored. We don't relish discomfort, but we recognize it for the disorienting dilemmas it creates: those cannonball moments. Our stories reconcile when they help us remember and sift through the raw materials of our communal lives and make decisions that allow us to move forward together.

Conclusion: A Pilgrim Story

We nearly missed the chapel.

It was tucked away, just off the path, in a small grove of trees. A much larger building made of stone and time had consumed the tiny chapel in its shadow. It seemed like the last gasp of the town we'd just passed through, a few shops and homes and not much else. The chapel was one final effort to say, "Hey, wait, stop here. Have a look."

The entrance was on the opposite side from our approach, and had there not been a long line of other pilgrims waiting their turn to step inside, we might have passed it by altogether, heads bent, eyes set on the dirt path ahead. We had already gotten all the stamps we needed for the day.

But there was a bit of mystery here, something hidden, beckoning us inward. Perhaps it was the soft church music that played from a hidden speaker. It was a respite in the forest shade and shadows. The chapel was dedicated to Mary Magdalene, so we thought it best to stop and give that saint her due.

Walking sticks in hand, Alli and I hefted our backpacks and headed for the growing line of fellow pilgrims, our respective scallop shells—that all-important symbol of the pilgrim—clanging against our empty water bottles.

We were on our second day of pilgrimage across northern Spain, walking the Camino de Santiago. It's an ancient route that begins in

France and ends in Santiago de Compostela, understood to be the final resting place of Santiago, better known to the English-speaking world as the apostle Saint James. Along with Rome and Jerusalem, Santiago de Compostela is considered to be a holy city in the Christian tradition and the ultimate geographic destination of countless pilgrims.

Alli and I had begun our journey in Sarria, about five days' walk from Santiago, or one hundred kilometers, the minimum needed to officially complete the pilgrimage. Our parents could watch our toddler for only so long. To prove that we really were walking the kilometers we claimed, we got stamps along the way in our Pilgrim Passport. Stamps could be found in shops or churches, at certain landmarks and even random fruit carts. They were simple ink markings that reflected their source, building one after another into a storied array of ink-stained markings. I remember a particularly interesting stamp from a brewery we discovered along the path—or, more truthfully, I remember how much I enjoyed that surprise bottle of beer early in the morning. You needed to collect at least two stamps each day of your walk.

The scallop shell that adorned our backpacks designated us as pilgrims. Along the way, bright yellow scallop shells emblazoned on small headstones guided us as we trekked across farmlands and into forests, past ancient churches and through vibrant towns. If the scallop-shell symbol was lacking, we often discovered instead bright yellow arrows painted on walls and signs and trees and any flat surface to help us find our way.

A pilgrimage is more than a trip to a destination; it's a spiritual journey, made with attentiveness and, for many, prayer. Sometimes the important part of the day lies off the predetermined path; we have to pay attention to what attracts us. Often, God is waiting for us just over the hill, a bit further off than what the map would suggest.

Thus, we found ourselves in line for a stamp at that little chapel dedicated to Mary Magdalene.

"This is taking a long time," I said. Alli nodded. The chapel wasn't much to behold: a statue of Mary, some candles, and the speaker. It was all rock and stone and darkness inside. A hush fell over the pilgrims as they stepped in, so we were grateful for the gentle music. It was a helpful distraction from the solitary man who, standing behind a table, kept describing every action he took as he stamped pilgrim passports.

"It's a little too tight in here for me," Alli said. "I'll let you get this stamp. I'll meet you outside."

I nodded, and she went back out into the early morning mist. There were still two pilgrims in front of me, and I was losing my patience. *So much for that great spiritual awakening.*

The man stamping passports wore a rather thick sweater. *He must be hot*, I thought, wishing that I, too, was outside with Alli. The air in this little space was still. But I'd come this far; I'd see it through.

The man was talking to the woman in front of me now, going on about how the stamp worked and the various colors she could choose from. It was a tough conversation, as he spoke in mumbled Spanish and the woman clearly did not. Finally, he took her hand, placed it on the stamp and waited. She moved the stamp to a place in her passport with an empty box, and together, they pressed down, ink materializing on the page.

That's odd, I thought. *She might as well just stamp it herself. Why is he doing it with her?*

It was my turn. I stepped up, allowed him to take my hand. I wasn't quite able to follow what he was saying, but I mirrored what the woman before me had done.

I felt a tap on my shoulder, then looked into the face of another woman, who touched her own eyes and then pointed to the man.

He's blind. This realization changed everything about that moment: the soft music, the shadows, the claustrophobia of the tiny chapel. And the gentle hand of this stranger who was grasping into darkness, trusting that there would be a hand of a fellow pilgrim to meet his own. And that together, he and that pilgrim would mark the suddenly sacred moment of spiritual journeying with a splash of colorful ink, then go separate ways.

Saint Ignatius considered himself a pilgrim from the moment of his conversion to the end of his life. In his autobiography, dictated from the future saint to one of his fellow Jesuits, he referred to himself only as "the pilgrim."

As we come to the end of our extended reflection on Ignatian storytelling, I find this image of the pilgrim to be essential. We know where our life begins and where it ends, no? A tiny cluster of cells to a pile of ash and bones. Birth and then death. Each and every one of us. There are no exceptions. We enter the world; we leave it. And for those of us of a religious persuasion, we take that one step further: we look to what comes next, after death, our ultimate encounter with the divine.

That's a boring story, though, isn't it? In fact, it inspires nothing but apathy. "Well," we may say, "there's nothing to be done. We all know how this thing ends. Just make the most of it while we're here. If it's not great now, maybe it'll be better in whatever comes next."

The pilgrim, though, knows that it's not just about getting to the final destination. It's about what happens along the way. The people we meet. The good we do. The surprises we allow ourselves to experience and that we give to others. It's about what we carry with us and how we carry it. It's about the realizations and the joys and the setbacks we encounter along the way. It's about what we build together. It's also about recognizing that we're not the only ones on the path: many have come before us, and many will follow us. Our footprints sink into the ground, atop the prints left by others, only to be trampled over the next day. The legacies we make, however humble, matter for the people who follow us. We all stumble forward, following those little yellow arrows as best we can, determined to see what comes next.

Ignatian storytelling is the process through which we bless those moments along the way. We dust them off and hold them up as sacred. We invite others to take a look, to make sense of what we've found. And we look, too, at what our neighbors have discovered. We make sense of it together. Maybe, too, in that sense-making we learn how to better set the path, make the markings more visible or push aside some fallen debris. We call out to those who have wandered into the woods, welcoming them back.

Despite the seemingly preordained nature of the path, each pilgrimage is existentially different. I remember how frustrated I was that our pilgrimage was only five days.

"We haven't really *done* the Camino de Santiago," I complained to Alli.

"I'm already excited to come back," was her response, hardly a day into the walk.

It wasn't until we had lunch with a few friends who had moved from Baltimore to Santiago at the end of our journey that we were set right. "Congratulations," they said. "You completed a Camino!"

I nodded, sheepishly, digging into my tortilla. "Well, not the whole thing." These two were pros. The one had walked the Camino countless times.

"You did *a* Camino," was the response. "Your Camino."

Indeed, these journeys are different. There would be little worth reconciling if we were all exactly the same. We'd need only one person to walk the path of healing and then yell out instructions to the rest of us. And what a boring world it would be.

As we reflect on ourselves as pilgrim storytellers, let us not lose sight of the value inherent in each of our stories. Unique though they are, they're part of the same web of story threads. Our role can be one of weaver: making sense of our stories, helping bring them together, building on one another and adding to the mystery of life.

If we want to live together peacefully in God's great human family, striving for what is good and wonderful, then we have no choice but to encourage one another in our respective stories. Like pilgrims on the Camino de Santiago, let us point out those little yellow arrows, helping one another forward, one slow step at a time. Let us not lose sight of those markers, even if we think our pilgrimage complete.

And sometimes, perhaps every time, it's worth adding an extra chapter, stepping off the dirt path to be surprised, to be humbled, to learn something new about what it means to be alive.

Acknowledgments

This book has been an opportunity for me to reflect on the many stories that make up my life and, more significantly, the many people who inspire and shape those stories. As I said at the outset, the power of stories lies in their ability to connect us. And so, I'd like to name just a few of the connections that made this book possible.

My colleagues and friends at both Catholic Relief Services and the Jesuit Conference of Canada and the United States who encouraged me in my storytelling—and sent me out into God's world to find and share stories of mission and meaning.

The team at Loyola Press—especially Vinita Hampton Wright and Gary Jansen—for their careful and patient shepherding of my ideas and words.

My longtime friend and spiritual director, Father James Bowler, SJ, who has helped me discover God at work in my story, as well as my communities at Fairfield University and Saint Ignatius Church Baltimore, for nurturing my Ignatian roots.

My parents and brother, my extended family, particularly my two grandmothers, who passed away during this project—Barbara Clayton and Camilla Jebran—who have guided and encouraged me in my life's story for thirty-two years.

My two daughters, Elianna and Camira, for the stories they stir in me each day.

And my wife, Alli, who continues to inspire me, who read each word with honesty, enthusiasm, and love—and whose support always gets me across the finish line.

Thank you.

Endnotes

1. Pope's Message for World Communications Day, https://www.vaticannews.va/en/pope/news/2020-01/ message-world-day-communication-life-history.html

2. Marshall Ganz, "Public Narrative" in *Accountability through Public Opinion*, 277.

3. Ibid., 275.

4. Simon Sinek, "How Great Leaders Inspire Action," May 6, 2010, https://www.ted.com/talks/ simon_sinek_how_great_leaders_inspire_action?language=en.

5. Dean Brackley, SJ, *The Call to Discernment in Troubled Times: New Perspectives on the Transformative Wisdom of Ignatius of Loyola* (New York: Crossroad Publishing Company, 2004), 49–50.

6. Ibid., 48.

7. Saint Ignatius of Loyola, *Personal Writings*, trans. Joseph A. Munitiz (New York: Penguin Putnam, 1996), 13.

8. Ibid., 261.

9. https://www.starwars.com/news/ studying-skywalkers-figuratively-exploring-the-dagobah-cave.

10. Marshall Ganz, "Public Narrative" in *Accountability through Public Opinion*, 285.

11. Saint Ignatius, *Personal Writings*, 289.

12. https://www.library.georgetown.edu/woodstock/ignatius-letters/ letter8.

13. Ibid.

14. Saint Ignatius of Loyola, *Spiritual Exercises*, 13th Annotation, in Saint Ignatius of Loyola, *Personal Writings*, trans. Joseph A. Munitiz (New York: Penguin Putnam, 1996), 285.

15. Spoken by Galadriel in the prologue of the film.

16. Marshall Ganz, "Public Narrative" in *Accountability through Public Opinion*, 285.

17. Lao Tzu, *Tao Te Ching*, chapter 13, https://www.wussu.com/laotzu/laotzu13.html, emphasis added.

18. Saint Ignatius, *Personal Writings*, 289.

19. Lao Tzu, *Tao Te Ching*, chapter 13, https://www.wussu.com/laotzu/laotzu13.html.

20. Thomas Merton, *Thoughts in Solitude* (New York: Farrar, Straus and Giroux, 1956, 1958), 79.

About the Author

Eric Clayton is the deputy director of communications at the Jesuit Conference of Canada and the United States. He joined the team in 2019 and produces content that shares the wide-ranging impact and opportunity of Ignatian spirituality. He also guest hosts *AMDG: A Jesuit Podcast*.

He previously worked at Catholic Relief Services, most recently as the campaign content manager, overseeing the development of prayer and advocacy resources aimed at promoting Catholic social teaching to a US-based audience. He has also managed social media channels for Maryknoll Lay Missioners, developed and directed retreats for the Sisters of Bon Secours, and was an adjunct professor in the Mass Communication department at Towson University. His writing has appeared in *America, National Catholic Reporter, Busted Halo, Amendo, Sojourners, Grotto Network, Give Us This Day*, and more.

He has a BA in creative writing and international studies from Fairfield University and an MA in international media from American University. He lives in Baltimore, Maryland, with his wife and two young daughters.

MORE BOOKS ABOUT **IGNATIAN SPIRITUALITY**

What Is Ignatian Spirituality?
Experiencing the Spiritual Exercises
of St. Ignatius in Daily Life

DAVID L. FLEMING, SJ

In *What Is Ignatian Spirituality?* David L. Fleming, SJ,
provides an authoritative yet highly accessible summary
of the key elements of Ignatian spirituality, among which
are contemplative prayer, discernment, and dynamic
involvement in service and mission.

In twenty concise chapters, Fr. Fleming explains how
this centuries-old method of disciplined reflection on
God's work in the world can deepen our spiritual lives
today and guide all the decisions we make.

English: Paperback I 978-0-8294-2718-9 I $14.99
Spanish: Paperback I 978-0-8294-3883-3 I $12.95

Ignatian Spirituality A to Z

JIM MANNEY

With *Ignatian Spirituality A to Z*, Jim Manney has
developed a brief, informative, and entertaining guide
to key concepts of Ignatian spirituality and essential
characters and events in Jesuit history. From Pedro
Arrupe to Francis Xavier, from Ad Majorem Dei Gloriam
to Zeal, this book uncovers the rich language of the
Jesuits. It will be an indispensable tool to anyone
interested in Ignatian spirituality, to staff, faculty, and
students at Jesuit institutions and schools, and to clergy
and spiritual directors who advise others about prayer
and spiritual matters.

Paperback I 978-0-8294-4598-5 I $14.95

TO ORDER: Call **800.621.1008**, visit **store.loyolapress.com**, or visit your local bookseller.

MORE BOOKS ABOUT **IGNATIAN SPIRITUALITY**

A Simple, Life-Changing Prayer
Discovering the Power of St. Ignatius Loyola's Examen

JIM MANNEY

In *A Simple, Life-Changing Prayer*, Jim Manney introduces Christians to a 500-year-old form of prayer—the Examen. St. Ignatius Loyola developed the Examen for the purpose of nurturing a reflective habit of mind constantly attuned to God's presence.

By following five simple yet powerful steps for praying the Examen, we can encounter the God whose presence in our lives can make all the difference in the world.

English: Paperback | 978-0-8294-3535-1 | $9.95
Spanish: Paperback | 978-0-8294-4389-9 | $9.95

Reimagining the Ignatian Examen
Fresh Ways to Pray from Your Day

MARK E. THIBODEAUX, SJ

Join Father Thibodeaux as he guides you through new and unique versions of the Examen, totally flexible and adaptable to your life. In ten minutes, you can tailor your daily prayer practice to fit your personal and situational needs, further enhancing and deepening your meditation.

Reimagining the Ignatian Examen will lead you through fresh and stimulating reflection on your past day, your present state of being, and your spiritual desires and needs for tomorrow.

English: Paperback | 978-0-8294-4244-1 | $13.99
Spanish: Paperback | 978-0-8294-4512-1 | $12.95

Also available as a free app for download on iOS and Android.

TO ORDER: Call **800.621.1008**, visit **store.loyolapress.com**, or visit your local bookseller.